THE BABYSITTER'S SURVIVAL GUIDE

FUN GAMES, COOL CRAFTS, SAFETY TIPS, AND MORE!

BY JILL D. CHASSÉ, PhD

STERLING CHILDREN'S BOOKS
New York

DEDICATED TO THE TWO WHO TEACH ME OODLES ABOUT CHILD DEVELOPMENT ON A
DAILY BASIS: MY SON, MALACHI ALEXEI, AND DAUGHTER, AVA MAE. — J. C.

STERLING CHILDREN'S BOOKS
New York

An Imprint of Sterling Publishing Co., Inc.
1166 Avenue of the Americas
New York, NY 10036

Library of Congress Cataloging-in-Publication Data
ISBN 978-1-4549-2318-3
Chassé, Jill D.
The babysitter's survival guide : fun games, cool crafts, and how to be the
best babysitter in town / Jill D. Chassé ; illustrated by Jessica Secheret.
p. cm.
Includes bibliographical references and index.
ISBN 978-1-4027-4654-3 (hc-plc concealed spiral : alk. paper)
1. Babysitting--Handbooks, manuals, etc. I. Secheret, Jessica. II. Title.
HQ769.5.C53 2010
649'.10248--dc22
        2009002538

Distributed in Canada by Sterling Publishing Co., Inc.
c/o Canadian Manda Group, 664 Annette Street
Toronto, Ontario, Canada M6S 2C8
Distributed in the United Kingdom by GMC Distribution Services
Castle Place, 166 High Street, Lewes, East Sussex, England BN7 1XU
Distributed in Australia by NewSouth Books
45 Beach Street, Coogee, NSW 2034, Australia

For information about custom editions, special sales, and premium and corporate purchases, please contact Sterling Special
Sales at 800-805-5489 or specialsales@sterlingpublishing.com.

Manufactured in China

Lot #:
2 4 6 8 10 9 7 5 3 1
07/17

www.sterlingpublishing.com

Art by Jeanine Murch
Design by Heather Kelly

CONTENTS

1   HOW TO RUN YOUR BUSINESS.. 1

2   THE INTERVIEW... 9

3   GETTING THE INFORMATION YOU NEED................................ 13

4   WHAT TO EXPECT FROM CHILDREN OF DIFFERENT AGES.............. 23

5   COMFORTING KIDS... 37

6   FIGHTING.. 48

7   ACTIVITIES AND CRAFTS... 54

8   TIME TO EAT... 67

9   BATH TIME... 81

10   BEDTIME.. 85

11   BABYSITTING CHILDREN WITH SPECIAL NEEDS.................. 90

12   PROBLEMS YOU MAY ENCOUNTER... 94

     CONCLUSION... 99

     BIBLIOGRAPHY... 101

     ABOUT THE AUTHOR.. 103

     INDEX.. 105

     BABYSITTING SCHEDULES.. 107

     MAKE YOUR OWN BUSINESS CARDS!.................................. 111

     CHILD INFORMATION SHEETS... 115

     EMERGENCY INFORMATION SHEETS.................................... 121

1

HOW TO RUN YOUR BUSINESS

IS BABYSITTING RIGHT FOR ME?

I like kids. I need money. I want to babysit! How do I find jobs?

Babysitting, like any other job, takes some work to find. It is important to market yourself for the type of babysitting position that you want.

First, decide if you have the skills needed to be a babysitter. A babysitter must be mature, responsible, able to react effectively in case of an emergency, and aware of young children's needs.

If you feel you meet these requirements, determine what age of children you want to work with. Do you like infants, preschoolers, or eight-year-olds? Think about where you have the most experience. Do you have a three-year-old cousin you always watch, or a baby sister that you often feed and diaper? Make a list of all the experience you have with children. This list is the first step in creating your babysitting résumé!

PUTTING YOUR RÉSUMÉ TOGETHER

First things first: Who are you? Create a new document on your computer, and at the top of the page, type your name, address, phone number, and e-mail address. This will tell prospective clients not only how to contact you, but how far away you live—an important factor if they may have to drive you home after a babysitting job.

Next you should write what is called an *objective*. This is your goal—what you are looking for in a babysitting job. Your objective highlights and summarizes your main qualifications and specifies the type of job you are looking for.

Here's an example objective: "A position as a babysitter for one to three children, ages six months to five years."

Then you'll want to include a line about when you're available.

For example: "Available: Monday–Thursday, 3–8 p.m.; Friday and Saturday nights, 4 p.m.–midnight."

Next, list your experience.

Here's an example: "May 2015–September 2016: Babysat my three cousins, currently ages three, five, and eight. Designed art projects and spent afternoons in the park."

Finally, you need references. Your references may be parents you babysat for in the past or teachers who know you well. Whomever you decide on, make sure to ask first if they would mind being contacted. Getting permission is very important, and you're more likely to get a good recommendation from someone who has had time to think about it and prepare.

A letter, signed by your reference, is the most professional way to present your references to your clients. If you are unable to get a reference letter, you should ask your references to be available by e-mail or phone. If they have agreed to be available by phone, find out what the best hours are to reach them.

If you know your references are busy, you may want to ask them to send you a two- or three-line reference e-mail that you can just save and forward to any babysitting clients you may have in the future.

Whether it's through a letter, phone call, or e-mail, encourage your references to mention the following:

- Who they are and how they know you (a neighbor, a client, a teacher, etc.)
- How long they have known you ("since summer of 2015" or "for four years")
- Things you have done that show you are qualified to babysit (taught kids new songs, helped baby learn to walk, etc.)

Some of your references may ask that you not include their information on your résumé but rather provide it only to people who ask for it. If this occurs, you may want to write "references available upon request" on your résumé and create a separate reference sheet to hand out if you are asked for it. If you do create a separate sheet, be sure to include your own contact information at the top. That way if it gets separated from your résumé, the potential client will still know whose references they have.

Whether you include references on your résumé or on a separate sheet, the information you provide will be the same: the name of your reference, phone number and/or e-mail address, the ages of the children you watched (if the reference is a client), and the dates of employment (again, if the reference is a client; if not, include how the person knows you and how long they have known you). It's also a good idea to include the address of any previous client who is serving as a reference. This will tell the parents what neighborhoods you have worked in and are familiar with.

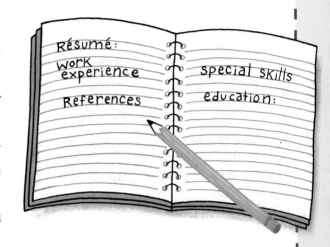

Here's a sample entry:

MR. AND MRS. SMITH
634 Cranberry Lane
Willard, NY 10362
(827) 555-9776
Ages of children: currently two and four
Dates employed: summer of 2016

Be sure to carry extra copies of your reference sheet and résumé whenever you go on an interview.

On the next page you'll find a sample of a completed résumé.

RÉSUMÉ

Joey A. Lopez
123 Pine Drive
Cedar, NJ 07019
(973) 555-4567
JALsitter@gmail.com

OBJECTIVE

A position as a babysitter for one to three children, ages six months to five years

EXPERIENCE

May 2015–September 2016: Babysat my three cousins, currently ages three, five, and eight. Helped with homework and spent afternoons at the pool.
Summer 2014: Babysat Smith children

REFERENCES

Mr. and Mrs. Smith
634 Cranberry Lane
Willard, NY 10362
(827) 555-9776
Ages of children: currently two and four
Date employed: summer of 2014

DETERMINING YOUR RATES

Before you can go into business, you need to decide what to charge for your services. The going rate is anywhere from minimum wage up to twice that amount, depending on your qualifications and the area you live in.

So what are your qualifications? Have you been babysitting for years? Can you get yourself to and from a babysitting job? Have you taken a babysitting course, or a first-aid or CPR class? These are all important factors and can bump up your asking price.

But they aren't the only factors to consider. Will you charge more for babysitting multiple children or for taking care of an infant? Is there an extra charge if the parents are out beyond your regular hours of availability?

You don't have to advertise all of these factors—just choose a rate that sounds reasonable based on your experience, but be prepared to discuss rates with potential clients during the interview.

Before deciding on your final rate, be sure to look at other advertisements that are posted around your neighborhood or online. You can also just ask your friends what they're charging. You may think that you're worth $12 an hour, but you don't want to lose the job because everyone else is charging only $9. Remember, babysitting is a business, and it pays to be competitive.

FIRST AID/CPR

If you plan to do a lot of babysitting, it would be a good idea to take a CPR and basic first-aid class. You'll be more confident when it comes to watching children, parents will trust you more, and you may even be able to charge more for your services.

Many local high schools, fire departments, and hospitals have classes that are not too expensive and can teach you these lifesaving techniques. The American Red Cross also provides a babysitting course that will further your knowledge of how to take care of children. Check out its website for details on how to sign up for a course online or in a classroom! Your local YMCA can be another great resource. Browse its website for any training opportunities.

Make sure you keep your course completion certificate in a safe place!

ADVERTISING YOUR NEW BUSINESS

Now that you're prepared to impress parents with your professional résumé and you've set your rates, it's time to let your customers know that you're out there. The best way to do that is by posting flyers, handing out business cards, and being active on social media! Keep in mind that you should be putting ads in places that parents visit often, whether they be physical or digital locations. Put a flyer in the local grocery store or on the community bulletin board, and keep business cards in your pocket or purse for parents that you might meet at the park, playground, or pool. Get in touch with the person who sends e-mail updates to the community and ask them if your babysitting ad can be part of the next e-mail sent to all residents. Chances are your community has a Facebook page. If so, you should check the page regularly for babysitter requests—and don't be shy about posting a brief ad!

So what should you put on your advertisements?

Well, it really depends on how much space you have. First and foremost, be sure to include a headline that will quickly allow parents to see what kind of job you are seeking. "Babysitting Service" at the top of the flyer, card, or online post will get the point across nicely. Secondly, you should always list your name, cell phone number, and e-mail address so that potential clients know how to contact you. It would also be a good idea to include your age or year in school, so that parents can decide if you are old enough to watch their children.

If you're creating a flyer or posting online, you'll have more room to include information about your experience. For example, you can write, "I have been babysitting for five years" or "I have CPR training." Anything that sets you apart from the other babysitters who are advertising their services is a plus.

Business cards provide you with less space to get your information across, so you'll have to choose the truly important facts. Your actual experience with children is the strongest information you can share with a parent, so list this first. This shows that you not only have the knowledge and experience, but also that you have enjoyed your time with kids enough to want to do it again and again! Always be sure to include your name and contact information, as well as the headline "Babysitter" or "Babysitting Service." If you have the room, you can include one additional fact from your flyer. Here is an example of what a business card might look like:

> # BABYSITTING SERVICE
> Rey Z. Lee
> Experienced babysitter for children ages 1–10
> High School Sophomore
> (578) 555-6423
> ReyZLee455@gmail.com

Flip to the back of this book to find tear-out business cards. Fill in the blanks with your information. You can also get business cards printed professionally at a local office supply store.

WHERE SHOULD I PUT MY FLYERS?

Local libraries, food stores, and community playgrounds are all excellent places to put up your flyers. Parents visit these locations often and are likely to see your advertisement. Local elementary schools and camps are also good places to post flyers, especially near the area where parents wait to pick up their kids. Remember to ask permission before you post your flyer! The last thing you want is to get in trouble for posting your flyers somewhere they shouldn't be.

OTHER WAYS TO GET THE WORD OUT?

Local or community papers, town LISTSERVs™, community websites, and local newsletters are distributed widely, and are therefore great places to advertise. Some of these offer free or cheap classified ads that will really help you get the word out. Also, look into the social groups that parents are a part of. Sometimes there are community-organized parent playdates at the mall, parent breakfast gatherings at a town center, or story times at the library—these are all places where you can leave your contact information.

BABYSITTING SERVICE!

REY Z. LEE

• Experienced babysitter for children ages 1-10
• High School Sophomore
Call: 578-555-6423
or ReyZLee455@email.com

SOCIAL MEDIA

Information travels fast online—use this to your advantage! You should ask your parents first before creating social media accounts, if you don't already have them. Here are some ways that you can advertise your babysitting service through social media:

- Tweet about it. If your community has a Twitter account, tag them. You just might get a retweet! It might even be worth it to create a Twitter account just for babysitting. Your handle could be something like: @SarahD_Babysitter.
- Post on Facebook. Posting on your community's Facebook page is one way to do it, but you could also try posting a status asking if anyone knows of a family in need of a babysitter. Chances are your friends babysit too, and they might be able to connect you with someone.
- Find a website or app. Do some research to find out if there is a babysitting website or app that is popular among parents in your community. Care and Sittercity are a couple of reputable sites that you can look into.

And finally, don't forget how important word of mouth is. Ask the parents you already babysit for to recommend you to their friends. You may even want to ask them if they will take a few of your business cards to hand out to other parents in need of a babysitter.

2

THE INTERVIEW

GET A JOB!

You've set up your résumé, put up a flyer, and received a phone call! Mr. and Mrs. Clark want to talk to you about watching little Kayla. Don't get nervous! As long as you are comfortable, prepared, honest, and presentable, you'll do great!

The most important thing you can do on an interview is to make a good impression. This is your chance to prove to the parents that they can trust you with their children. So here are a few things to remember:

- Arrive on time.
- Introduce yourself in a courteous manner.
- Wear something clean, presentable, and professional. Something that is appropriate for school should be just fine.

Remember that although the decision to hire you rests with the parents, this is as much your interview as it is theirs. It is your chance to decide if you feel comfortable working for this family, so ask questions. Find out the important information up front:

- How many children will you be watching and how old are they?
- Do any of the children have special needs?
- What days and hours will they want you to babysit?
- How will you get home after a job?
- What qualities are the parents looking for in a babysitter?

Then try to find out something about the children. "Is Kayla involved in any sports?" you can ask. They may say that she is on a soccer team. Now you know you can play soccer with her in the backyard and she'll have fun!

Use the children's names and ask things that are helpful and appropriate. Show a genuine interest and learn as much as you can about the children. Parents know their children better than anyone else. They will tell you important information that you wouldn't otherwise know. Perhaps their daughter always cries when they leave, but her special teddy bear will cheer her up, or their son will say he's allowed to play ball in the house, but that's not actually true.

Once you've learned what you can about the children, get to know the parents and what they're okay with. How would they feel about you bringing crafts and activities? Can you bring your homework? Is there anything they would like you to avoid while you are in their home? Perhaps they would prefer that you not go into the basement or answer the phone. It's important to ask so you'll know your boundaries.

Talk about your strengths and experience, but don't become self-absorbed or self-conscious. Be sure to keep your attention on the job and the child, not on yourself. For example, you may say: "I have been babysitting for three years, and I really love interacting with kids!" Or "Last year I took a water-safety class, so I feel comfortable taking children to the pool."

Be prepared to talk about the following points. Even if the parents don't ask, they are great things to discuss and show how prepared and experienced you are:

- Talk about any formal training that you've had, such as CPR and/or first-aid training.
- If you can swim, let the parents know. This is great for summer babysitting and it will make parents who have a pool feel more comfortable.
- Can you drive? Do you have a car? Have you driven children in it (and do you feel comfortable driving children)? How's your driving record? Also, make sure that the children have car seats available if you will be transporting them in your car. Always be sure they are buckled in correctly.
- How well do you know your way around the area? It's good for parents to know you won't get lost with the kids if you go out of the house or neighborhood for a walk or drive if they approve of those activities.
- Sometimes parents ask you to do some household tasks like laundry, dishes, shopping, cooking for children, etc. If this is okay with you, let them know. If not, it shouldn't interfere with your eligibility for the job, but you should be up-front and tell them.
- Be sure to mention any issues you may have with pets or any allergies.

After discussing the job, parents may ask about your rate. Be prepared to tell them what you charge per hour (or if you have a flat rate for the evening) and any special charges that you might need to include, such as charging an extra two dollars an hour for two kids instead of one, or extra for doing household tasks. This is also a good time to discuss how the parents plan to pay you (cash, check, or through an online payment service; after the job or before if you charge a flat fee).

When the interview is over, remember to thank the parents and tell them you look forward to hearing from them.

THINGS TO LOOK OUT FOR

The family you are meeting with will most often set the place for the interview. An interviewer should never take advantage of you. This includes asking you to have alcohol, making sexual advances, or suggesting a relationship or activity that is unprofessional. An interview should always take place in an appropriate setting, such as the living room or kitchen—not at the bar or in the bedroom. If the family suggests meeting in a place that does not feel right to you, it is okay to tell them that you don't feel comfortable with the choice and suggest an alternate location. If you do feel that an interviewer is taking advantage of you, politely excuse yourself and tell an adult.

3

GETTING THE INFORMATION YOU NEED

DRESSING THE PART

The interview went well and you got the job! Now what?

When you go on a babysitting job, you should wear something that looks presentable and appropriate but will allow you to be active and play with the kids. This means no sweats or ripped T-shirts—old or torn clothing might seem disrespectful to the parents. This also means no stockings and heels. It's difficult to run after a two-year-old while wearing stilettos, and someone is bound to get hurt!

Remember that you're probably going to get dirty, so don't wear your favorite cashmere sweater or new dress slacks. Try jeans or khakis with a polo or nice shirt. Don't wear dangling earrings when watching a child younger than two—they'll look like a fantastic toy to grab! The harder it is to pull on your clothing, the better off everyone will be.

MAKING A GOOD IMPRESSION

If you are being picked up by one of the parents, be sure you are ready to go at least ten minutes before the time discussed. If you're driving yourself or getting dropped off, arrive at the house on time. If this is your first time at that home, give yourself an extra ten to fifteen minutes to do a walk-through with the parents and become familiar with where things are.

If the children will be asleep for some of the time you're babysitting, bring something to do with you. This is true of most night jobs. If you're watching a three-year-old from 5:00 p.m. to 10:00 p.m., expect to play with the child until about 8:00 p.m. After that, you'll need to be prepared with homework, a laptop, or a book to read. If you bring homework or study materials, remember to bring them out only after the kids are put to bed, not when you should be watching them. It's fine to watch TV after the kids are asleep, but only if you get the parents' permission first. Before the parents leave, find out if it is okay for you to use the technology in the house. Usually, parents will leave written instructions for accessing the TV and Internet. If they don't or if you are unsure about what is off limits to you, just ask. Out of respect for the family's privacy, don't simply assume every electronic device is yours to tinker with.

WHAT SHOULD YOU KNOW BEFORE A PARENT LEAVES YOU ALONE?

The most important thing about babysitting is keeping the children safe. This is essentially your main purpose. Entertainment and education are always secondary to *safety*. Children need supervision at all times! You are fully responsible for the children when the parents are not there.

When you are in a new place, make sure you know the address. Have it in your cell phone and written down where you can access it in the case of an emergency, especially if your battery dies. Even if you know it by heart, write it down anyway. It is easy to forget when you're in a panic during an emergency situation. Also, be sure you have written down or saved in your phone the family's name, children's names, nearest cross streets, instructions on how to contact the parents, emergency phone numbers such as 9-1-1 in the United States and Canada to contact your local police and fire departments, the hospital, the phone numbers of the family's close relatives and neighbors, the doctor's name and phone number along with a medical release, and the number for Poison Control, which is (1-800) 222-1222 in the United States and Canada.

At the back of this book, you'll find Emergency Information Sheets, which are for writing down all this information. Keep one somewhere in the house where you'll have easy access to it and then copy the information into your phone.

In addition to this information, each time you babysit you should find out where the parents will be, how to contact them at that location, and when they are expected home.

CHILD INFORMATION SHEET

You should also ask the parent to go over the children's medical information with you. Are the children taking any medicine? If so, make certain you know how much and when it should be given. If you do have to give the medicine to the children, write down what you gave and when so the parents will know. Does the child have any allergies (particularly food allergies) that you should be aware of, such as gluten or lactose intolerance? Are there any other diet restrictions? As you gather information on the children you are watching, write it on a Child Information Sheet, like the ones provided

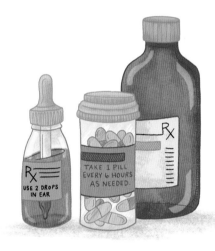

at the back of this book. This sheet contains not only important medical information, but a list of the child's likes and dislikes as well. As with the Emergency Information Sheets, you would fill out one card to keep in the house and also transfer the same information into your phone so you always have a digital copy with you.

Also, be sure the parents have your number and that you keep your phone on at all times you are with the children should they need to reach you. Emergencies can go both ways.

Remember, it's a lot easier to have fun with someone who knows you. Kids may be small, but they have their own personalities, likes and dislikes, preferences, and ideas. As their babysitter, it's important you know the little ins and outs of their personality so that both of you will enjoy your time together.

Many of a child's favorites can be learned through communication with the parents, which is why it's important to go over the Child Information Sheet with the parents before they leave. As you learn things like a favorite toy, movie, character, TV show, book, or song, add to the Child Information Sheet. Remember to make a different sheet for each of the kids you babysit and update it as you learn more about the child's likes and dislikes. The sheet is a good reference guide and will serve as a nice refresher the next time you babysit for the family.

THE WALK-THROUGH

Before the parents leave, do a walk-through of the house. Look for potential hazards in the home such as open stairways, uncovered electrical outlets, and sharp objects that are within reach. These aren't hazards for you, but could be an accident waiting to happen for a young child. Many parents have their house "babyproofed," meaning that the outlets are covered, stairs have baby gates on them, cabinets have child locks installed, etc. For the homes that have not been babyproofed, take all these hazards into consideration.

Find out where the parents keep the cleaning supplies and chemicals so you can keep the kids away from them, and locate the first-aid supplies in case someone does get hurt. At the very least, you should have bandages easily accessible. We will talk about addressing cuts, bruises, and injuries later on in this book.

Ask about candles and flashlights in case of a blackout while the parents are gone. Even if it looks bright and sunny out, a storm can hit at any time, and it's good to be prepared if you lose power. Also, ask what the fire-escape plan is. If there isn't one, be sure you know *all* the exits out of the home. Is there a back door? A porch? How would you exit from upstairs? Last of all, you should ask where the smoke alarms and fire extinguishers are. If you don't know how to use the fire extinguisher, have an adult show you before you are alone in the house with the children.

HOUSE RULES

Once you've finished the walk-through, be sure to go over the house rules for both you and the children. You need to know what the rules are so that you can comply and make sure the children are doing what they are supposed to do. House rules can be simple tasks like taking off your shoes when you come inside, shutting all the doors in the house when the air conditioning is on, or never putting your feet up on the couch. These rules are important to a family and a household, so it's best to learn and respect them when you are a guest in the house. Some of the more common ones include:

HOMEWORK

If the child is old enough to have homework, there are usually a lot of rules associated with this task. Do they have to finish it before playing? Do they get to do their homework at the kitchen table or does it have to be in their room? Parents usually have these rules locked in, so just ask if there are any homework rules and they'll let you know.

SCREEN TIME

You'll probably run into screen time and electronics rules no matter what age the child is. Between iPads, video games, phones, and TV, kids have a plethora of electronics to keep them busy.

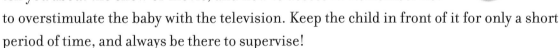

Generally, parents don't want their children to be stuck in front of a screen and may bring up this point. There are some infant/toddler video programs that a family may approve. If this is the case, they'll probably tell you about the show or movie, and how to access it. Remember not to overstimulate the baby with the television. Keep the child in front of it for only a short period of time, and always be there to supervise!

As children get older, they may want to watch a special show or movie. Or, they may be attached to a specific game on an electronic gaming device. Children can be very vocal about their opinions and choices when it comes to electronics—but that doesn't always mean you should listen. Ask the parents first if the child can have screen time, what they are allowed to watch or play, and for how long. Maybe the child is allowed to play the gaming system for fifteen minutes before dinner and can't be in front of a screen at all after 7:00 p.m. If the child has their own cell phone, make sure you know the rules associated with it. Maybe

calls can only be made after homework is done, or they cannot download any apps. The parents are ultimately responsible for setting time limits, schedules, and restrictions for electronics, but as the babysitter it's your job to enforce those rules.

You should also find out what your own screen privileges are. When are you allowed to use the family's cable, Internet, movie-streaming, or on-demand services? Would parents prefer that you only do so once the children are soundly asleep? Even if the parents don't say anything about it up-front, it's best to stay off your phone unless you are contacting the parents. You don't want their children to report later that you were texting your friends the whole time.

PICTURES

You may want to snap selfies with the kids you're watching or take silly pictures when they're in the pool, but check with the parents before posting or tagging their kids on social media. Posting pictures of children can carry a risk and many parents do not want such images posted publicly. If it's okay with the parents, they might want you to text them pictures of the kids playing so they can see that their little ones are having fun while they are out. You can even video chat with the parents if you have a younger child that gets sad, scared, or lonely. Seeing their mom or dad could help reassure them in a moment of anxiety.

FIRE SAFETY

Once the parents leave, discuss or practice fire safety with the children. Many families have a designated meeting place outside the house. Both you and the children need to know where it is in case you lose track of one another during a fire. If they don't have a predetermined spot, come up with an easy one like "the mailbox at the end of the driveway" or "the apple tree by the curb." If the child is old enough to walk, tell them to *get out*, *stay out*, *do not hide*, and meet at the special spot. Count heads when you're there to make sure you've got everyone.

Inside the house, you can practice staying *low* to the ground, feeling a door for heat *before* opening it, and *stopping*, *dropping*, and *rolling* if any part of the child catches on fire. If there *is* a fire in the house:

- Yell "FIRE!" as loud as you can, and gather the children.
- *Get out* of the house—don't try to put out the fire. Go to the designated meeting spot.
- Once you have all the children, go to a neighbor's house and call 9-1-1. Then call the parents.
- Don't go back inside!

USING THE TELEPHONE

If there is a landline in the house, find out if the parents want you to answer it or let it go to voicemail. If so, how should you answer? "Smith residence" or simply "Hello?" Remember not to offer any information on the phone and not to tell anyone you're alone. Also, check to see if the children are allowed to answer and/or use the phone. This is especially applicable for older kids in elementary school who tend to use the phone when their parents are home.

ANSWERING THE DOOR

Ask the parents before they leave if they are expecting anyone to stop by. Find out if they have a procedure for answering the door or rules they want you to follow, such as looking through the window first or not opening the door after 9:00 p.m. You shouldn't be letting anyone in the house unless it's been prearranged by the parents.

AT THE END OF THE JOB

PAYMENT

Before the parents come home, figure out how much they owe you for your services. Be prepared to make change for them if need be.

Although a rare situation, the parents might say they can't pay you right away. They may be out of cash or thought that you would accept a check, but maybe you don't have a checking account. These issues should be taken care of when initially setting up the job, but if it does occur, find out how they intend on paying you. If the parents say that they have to pay you another time, ask for an IOU. A written and signed note would qualify.

If a week passes and they still do not pay you, or if they have a habit of not paying on time, talk to your parents. It is also helpful to have another adult present when you speak to your employer about the situation. The parents hired you with the understanding that they would pay you at the end of the job. If they repeatedly fail to do so, you should terminate your relationship.

WHAT IF THE PARENTS ARE LATE COMING HOME?

Sometimes parents show up late because of circumstances beyond their control. If it's more than fifteen minutes past the time they told you they would be home, you should text them or give them a call. Fifteen to twenty minutes is a reasonable amount of time to wait, in case there was traffic or an accident on the route they take home.

If over an hour passes and you can't reach the parents, call the emergency number they left (it may be a neighbor, a family friend, or a relative) and explain the situation to that person. Make sure you also tell your parents that your employer is late and that you will be coming home at a later time than expected.

ADDITIONAL SAFETY TIPS

- If it is evening, turn on the porch/outside light, and keep the window shades closed and the doors locked.
- *Do not* open the door for anyone. If someone insists on coming in and you do not recognize that person, or if you suspect something is wrong, *do not let them in*. Call 9-1-1.
- If the children are awake, know their location at all times and never leave them alone too long.
- If the children are asleep, check in on them every fifteen to twenty minutes to make sure they are still in their beds.
- Never leave a baby unattended on a changing table, bed, or high chair. Babies don't understand the danger of heights, and once they learn how to roll (at about four months old), they keep moving! Babies love to practice their new skills, but they need to practice in a safe place. Even if they can't crawl yet, babies can easily roll off of a changing table or bed the second you turn your back. In a high chair, a little squirmer can slither under the tray and fall right onto the floor. To avoid this, use safety straps whenever they are available.
- Never leave a child unattended in the bathtub. Baths are even more dangerous than changing tables, beds, and high chairs. A child can drown in just an inch of water. Even if it looks like the baby is sitting well in the tub, it only takes a moment to slip and go headfirst into the water. Even an older child can slip in a bathtub.
- Keep a close watch on a baby in a walker. The baby may seem very independent in their walker, but they have no idea if they're headed down the stairs or into the fireplace. It's up to you to keep them out of harm's way. Let them practice running those little legs in a risk-free zone, like an open playroom or den with no pointy table edges to run into.

- If for any reason you must leave the house, *take the children with you!*
- If the parents have given you permission to take the children out of the house, make sure you have a house key with you when you leave. Double-check that all doors and windows are locked. Also, make sure that the children go to the bathroom before leaving. This will help to avoid accidents or having to use public restrooms.

It is okay to ask the parents to give you a call or text if they are going to be running late. If they are consistently late, you may want to consider not working for them anymore, but remember, be polite and explain the problem you have with their lateness. They may correct this behavior or they may say they will find another sitter. Either way, do your best to stay on good terms. The last thing you want is for them to tell other parents that you were unprofessional.

GETTING HOME

If you do not drive, it is important to find out how you'll be getting back home after your babysitting job. Often, parents will provide this transportation, but don't assume they will drive you. Ask beforehand so you can plan alternate transportation if necessary. Even if you are within walking distance, some parents would rather take you home, especially if the job ends late in the evening. Others will trust you to find your own way home. Whatever the plan, always make sure you have an alternate way to get home.

If the parent agrees to take you home, but appears intoxicated, don't accept a ride with them. It is okay to politely refuse and call your backup transportation.

BEYOND REGULAR BABYSITTING

Some parents like to do co-op babysitting or nanny shares with their friends. How comfortable are you with occasional doubling up or watching kids from two or three families? Do you have experience watching several children at once? Turn to page 34 for information on how to handle payment in this type of a situation.

At times parents may also ask you to go on vacation with them. Vacation babysitting can be a fun and rewarding experience. It gives parents some free time, and makes time together with the family less stressful since a babysitter can help out. It's also a chance for you to relax a little and get away while getting paid and doing what you enjoy. If this is something that interests you, let them know.

Pricing for vacation babysitting may run a little differently than your typical evening at their home. Some parents will offer a flat rate for a trip, while others will continue to pay hourly. A suggestion for a vacation price would be to take your hourly rate and multiply it by eight hours each day. For example, if you are making $12 an hour, that would charge $96 a day. If you take a trip with a family for three days, the total would be $288. You might not work a full eight-hour shift like you would at a store or office, but the cost analysis is about the same.

When you're planning to go on vacation with a family, make sure you discuss break times and free time for yourself. Before you agree to go, ask the parents what hours they expect you to be available to watch the kids. Also, find out if you will be on your own for meals or if you'll be eating with the family. If they are paying for your meals, lodging, and/or travel, you might consider charging them less for babysitting.

WHAT TO EXPECT FROM CHILDREN OF DIFFERENT AGES

PREPARE YOURSELF

Before you're alone with the kids, you should know what to expect. Here's a breakdown of different ages and the behavior you will most likely see, as well as some activities specific to each age group.

INFANTS (NEWBORN–ONE YEAR)

Babies are not only capable of interacting and playing, but they learn and soak up loads of new information to help their brains grow as you play with them. Babies also need a lot of attention. When they cry, there's a reason. It's okay to hold them and pick them up. This is how they learn to trust and learn about the world. Crying is also how they communicate. They could be saying they are hungry, have a dirty diaper, or just want love because they miss their parents.

For newborns, good activities involve calm and gentle games. During the first month they prefer looking at contrasting colors, like black, white, and red. If the parents don't have any newborn books available, it is nice to bring your own to share and read. Newborns also like mirrors and watching themselves. A great thing to do with a mirror is to look in it with the baby and make silly faces. Babies are attentive to exaggerated expressions like a really big smile or a big sad frown. Make silly faces in the mirror and tell the baby what you're doing. "A big smile for Emma!" "Look at Kallie's frown. Is Kallie sad?"

Music, soft lullabies, and children's songs are great to play for a new baby as well. Babies especially love when you sing to them. Simple kids' songs like "Twinkle, Twinkle, Little Star" or "The Itsy Bitsy Spider" are great. You can even put the radio on, hold the baby, and dance gently while singing to them.

At two months a baby's vision will allow them to find interest in more colorful and complex pictures and toys. Pick out a book and open it in front of the baby. Point out different items and make silly sounds to go with each item, such as "This is a cow—a cow says *moooooo*!" If the baby starts to babble with you, use the sounds they're making and repeat them to help encourage their speech.

At three months, babies become more social and interactive. They start to prefer games that involve tugging and grasping. Find a rattle or some other toy that makes a sound.

HOLDING A BABY

When you pick up an infant from their crib or bassinet, it is *very important* to support the *head*. Slide one hand under the child's neck and open your fingers so that your hand can support the whole head. Slide your other hand under the baby's lower back or between their legs. This is the hand that will be holding the weight of the baby. The hand under the baby's head is for supporting the neck only. Make sure you are holding the baby around the torso. When your hands feel secure, lift up the infant and hold them close to your body. You may want to practice at home with a doll.

Babies are sensitive and delicate. They need and want to be close to your body. Not only does that give them support, but it also gives them warmth and a healing human touch. Remember to keep the baby secure as a bundle. Support the head and keep the baby's body upright.

Gently shake the toy near one side of the baby. Then move it around their head and shake it again. Move it slowly from place to place and see if the baby will follow it with their eyes. If they try to touch the rattle, hold it within reaching distance and help them grasp it by putting it against their palm.

By four months old, a baby can usually hold up their head independently and practice early crawl movements, such as pushing up from a belly position. Eye contact and facial expressions are also important and can go a long way. Not only can you get their attention, but they will watch you and learn. They may giggle when you tickle them or take a toy from you. Babies at this age will begin to babble and imitate sounds.

Some fun activities you can do with a baby this age include:

TOUCH AND FEEL

Pick up the baby and walk into the living room. Go to the couch and tell them what it is. Next, have them touch it and tell them how it feels (say "soft"). Continue on throughout the room finding other interesting objects and textures. Be careful not to touch anything breakable.

PEEK-A-BOO OBJECT

Get a small bag that you cannot see through. Place some of the baby's favorite items inside. Sit facing the baby and pull the items out one by one. Say, "Look! It's your rattle!" Then hide it again in the bag. Ask the baby, "Where did the rattle go?" Wait a few moments, and then pull out the item again and say "Look! Here is your rattle!" Move on to another item. Do this with three or four items, or until the baby gets bored (looks away, seems disinterested, or starts to fidget or cry).

READING

Reading to a baby at this age helps language skills develop. Board books and picture books with bright colors are great, because they help stimulate babies' visual development.

By five or six months old, a baby will be able to sit up on their own. Babies at this age can grasp objects and even move them from one hand to the other. Direct interaction occurs more openly now, so talk face-to-face and make lots of facial expressions. Be attentive to the child's moods. Ask them questions like "Do you like this soft ball?" or "Does this applesauce taste sweet?" Use lots of descriptive words (color, taste, size, feel, shape, etc.). Remember to repeat, repeat, repeat. Other fun activities for this age include rolling a soft ball back and forth with the baby; giving the child a toy that rattles, jingles, or rings when you shake it; making music together (you can shake a noisy toy to a beat or some background music); and giving the baby a wet (wrung out, not soaking) washcloth and dry washcloth. Explain the difference ("This is wet. This is dry.") and let them feel each one.

Babies at this age also love to use their hands. Hold the baby's hand and show them how to do "Pat-a-Cake" or "The Itsy Bitsy Spider." Clap your hands then take the baby's hands and gently clap them together.

Eight to ten months is an exciting time for an infant. A baby at this age is becoming mobile! You'll have to keep up with them. Be sure that the parents have the house baby-proofed (covered outlets, locked cabinets, etc.) before you let the child wander. If they do not, you need to be especially cautious of these things.

Try these activities with an eight- to ten-month-old:

TRACING SHAPES

Find a colorful book or magazine. Put the baby on your lap and open up the book. Trace the shapes you find with your finger and describe what you see (for example, trace a beach ball and say "round"). Hold the baby's hand gently and trace the shape with their finger. Repeat twice with each object.

RATTLE DANCE

Turn on some music and get two rattles. Sit on the floor with the baby in front of you and shake the rattle to the beat of the music. Give the baby the other rattle and see if they'll shake it with you.

SOUND HUNT

Take the baby on a walk through the house. Find objects in each room that make noise, and repeat that noise (such as the clock in the bedroom, which makes a tick-tock noise, or the microwave in the kitchen, which makes a beeping sound).

OTHER GOOD ACTIVITIES

Other activities include stacking blocks or containers, scribbling with crayons on paper (another great item to bring if the parents don't have any), or making drums out of upside-down cups and spoons.

Between ten and twelve months, most babies will begin walking. Children at this age can usually recognize objects ("Where is the dog?" "Bring me your toy bunny."). Good activities include using a blanket, cups, or canisters in the playroom to hide some little toys, then asking the children to find them; pushing around toy cars and trucks (only big ones—larger than a toilet paper tube—until the kids are over three); or playing hand rhymes and songs such as "Pat-a-Cake," "The Itsy Bitsy Spider," and "Round and Round the Garden." If you're not familiar with these songs and rhymes, you may find it helpful to get a nursery rhyme or hand rhyme book from the library or bookstore, or watch a few children's shows to learn some fun play songs.

Another fun game to play is "Bicycle Trip." Lay the baby on their back and gently bend their little knees. Bring them up to their chest and back down again in a bicycle-pedaling motion. Make up a place you're going to ride to and pause pedaling to check out the sights. You could say, for example, "Let's ride our bike to the zoo! Pedal, pedal, pedal—look at those monkeys! Pedal, pedal, pedal . . . Wow! Check out the lion! Roar!" Think of all the make-believe places you can go!

At first you may feel silly talking to a baby since they can't talk back and may look confused, but they can hear and process what you're saying in their own way. They will become familiar with your voice and it will increase their security when you babysit again.

Remember that infants can't talk, so they may communicate through crying. As discussed earlier, crying can mean that they need a diaper change, they are hungry, or they just want to be held. The more time you spend with the baby, the easier it will be to understand their different cries. Did you know that a hungry cry sounds different than a dirty-diaper cry? It's almost as if babies have their own language. Also, look for other cues that go along with the cry, such as gnawing on their fingers or rubbing their eyes. There is a plethora of ways that a baby can talk to you via non-verbal communication.

TODDLERS (AGES ONE–TWO YEARS)

Toddlers are called toddlers because they toddle! This is the age when they start to become more independent, not only by learning to walk on their own, but also by making choices in what they want to play, eat, and do. They love to do things all by themselves. It's fun as a babysitter to offer the toddler several choices and let them decide. Let them pick between two games or decide which book they want to read. At this age children also love to get into everything, so keep an extra close watch on them!

Here are some activities that can keep toddlers entertained:

CEREAL DRAWINGS

Take a handful of small Os or puffed cereal and put it in a bowl on the table. Then get some kid-safe glue, crayons, and paper. Draw any items you can think of with missing circles, help the toddlers put glue on the cereal, and have the toddler fill the circles in with cereal. For example, draw some cars without wheels, and have the toddler put the cereal where the wheels would go.

PRETEND PARTY

Get a bunch of stuffed animals together and set up a table in an open play area. Pretend there's a birthday cake in the center of the table, and find "presents" from the child's toy box. Sing "Happy Birthday" to one of the stuffed animals and pretend to blow out candles on a cake. You can even make party hats and placemats out of construction paper. Toddlers love to color, so they can help to design these!

BLANKET TENT

Pretend you're going camping and make a tent inside the house! Drape a blanket over two chairs or a table. Throw a bunch of stuff inside the tent, such as books, pillows, and stuffed animals. Crawl into the tent with the child and pretend like you're camping in the wilderness!

Between fourteen and twenty months of age, a child will usually start to speak. They begin with simple words that they have heard often, such as "mama" or "dada." These words eventually turn into two-word phrases, which is the next step on the journey of speech. Two-word phrases such as "come baby" or "doggie gone" begin around the age of two years. By this point, a baby should have around fifty words in their vocabulary. When a child can link two words together, it shows an understanding of both words and content. Be sure to talk to the child and encourage them to talk back.

TERRIBLE TWOS!

They call this age the "terrible twos" because children at this age have a need for autonomy and also a very short attention span. It doesn't have to be "terrible," but it can certainly be a handful! When a toddler continually expresses their feelings in a negative way (bad mood, temper tantrums, etc.), they could be making a statement that they need your acknowledgment. Playing with them—not just watching them play—can help to prevent tantrums.

Two-year-old children are active, outgoing, and interested in more in-depth games and activities. Here are a few you can try!

NUMBER JUMP

Draw big numbers on construction paper. Cut them out and scatter them on the floor in the play area. Call out the numbers and have the child jump onto the paper number when you call it out.

PAPER RACES

Crumple up a bunch of pieces of paper and lay them out on a table. Sit the child at the table with a straw and ask them to blow the paper across the table. You sit across from the child and blow the paper balls back to them.

FREEZE DANCE

Turn the radio on and begin to dance. A few minutes after the music starts, yell "freeze" and turn off the music. The child has to stop moving completely in the position they were in when the music stopped. Hold it for a few seconds then turn the music on again. Repeat the freeze every few minutes throughout the song.

COLOR FISH FIND

Cut out a bunch of fish from different colored construction paper. Hide them all around the playroom or child's play area. When all are hidden, ask the child to find a fish then bring it to you and tell you the color. When the child has found all of the fish, line them up and say the colors together.

PRESCHOOLERS (AGES THREE–FOUR YEARS)

At this age, children are little social beings, interested in what everyone's doing and why. The way a child looks at the world and those around them has a significant impact on their development.

Preschoolers will start to copy this behavior and try to be like the grown-ups they see. Without a positive role model, children may acquire inappropriate behaviors from bad influences in a negative environment. This is why it is so important for you to be a positive role model! They are watching what you do and what you say. Kids at this age also like role-playing and make-believe dress-up games, like putting on Mommy's coat and shoes, or Daddy's favorite hat. Have some dramatic playtime with the child you are watching. Ask what they want to be, and find something around the house to help them pretend. Enter a make-believe world for a little while and allow the child to take on the part. If they want to be a doctor, bring them some stuffed animals so they can check the animals' temperatures, or put on bandages. If they want to be a teacher, set up a pretend classroom with their toys and give them a few grown-up books so they can pretend they are teaching.

Some other activities you can do with preschool-age kids include:

ANIMAL CHARADES

Fill a shoebox or paper bag with pictures of animals. Let the child pull out the pictures one at a time and act them out while you guess what they're doing. If there are other kids, let them try to guess what the animal is, too.

GUESS THE OBJECT

Collect a handful of kid-safe objects and put them in a pile on a table or the floor. Then get a small blanket and put it in front of the objects. Ask the child to close their eyes, then hide one of the objects under the blanket. Let the child feel the object under the blanket and try to determine what it is. If they can't guess it, give them easy hints ("It's red." "It goes fast.") until they figure it out.

ANIMAL RACES

Go into a wide-open space where it's okay to run around, like a playroom or backyard. Make a start and finish line, marked by a chair or stuffed animal. Put the child at the start and name an animal. The child then has to act like that animal all the way to the finish line. This one is great with more than one child, too. Remember to allow all the kids a chance to win. Some good animals for this game are turtles ("Can you crawl slowly?"), bunnies ("Hop! Hop! Hop!"), elephants ("Let me see that trunk!"), and bats ("Flap those wings!"). Think of animals that don't go too fast to reduce the risk of accidents!

GROCERY STORE

Pick some items from the kitchen and put them in a bag (not refrigerated stuff, which might go bad if you're playing for a long time). Have the child go behind a table like it's a checkout counter and come up to the counter with the items. Pretend to "check out" and ask how much each object is. Then ask the child "What can I do with this one?" If the child can't think of anything, give them some suggestions ("Can I make anything with it?" "Can I cook it?").

EARLY ELEMENTARY SCHOOL (AGES FIVE-SEVEN YEARS)

A younger child believes that rules are set in stone and cannot be altered. Older children understand that rules are developed by people, not some all-powerful force, and can be changed or amended. More important, they aren't afraid to test the rules. They also aren't afraid to tell you how they feel and express their joy or anger in having a babysitter. Be ready for this, and make sure to enforce the rules their parents set forth, no matter what the children might say.

Older kids often spend time with a group of similar kids going through similar experiences, such as a new baby sister or brother, Miss Jones's third-grade art class, or growth spurts. This peer group takes on a special significance. It offers a place between the world of grown-ups and that of babies. This is important for you, the babysitter, to understand, so you know what to talk to them about. Ask them questions about their friends, school subjects, or TV shows that they like to watch. Talk about when you were in first grade or second grade and what you remember about your favorite teacher, class, or friend.

Kids at this age are curious and intelligent enough to sit and learn, yet still very restless and fidgety, so it's good to have some activities planned for them. Some activities for this age are:

GAMES

There's nothing like a good old game night! Break out the chess or checkers, see if they know how to play Monopoly, or teach them Uno! Scrabble is another fun game for kids that are learning to spell. Board games are great for this age group as well as older children. You could even tweak the rules of a game a little to make an easier version for younger kids.

If you bring a deck of cards with you, you can introduce games such as Go Fish, Memory, Slap Jack, or War. Here are instructions for how to play some kid-friendly games:

GO FISH

This is a great game for younger kids who are learning their numbers. Hand out five cards to each player, placing them face down. Put the remaining cards in the center of the table or playing area, face down. Leave space in the center for a discard pile. The first player should pick one of their own cards that they want to find a match for. That player should then ask the player to their right, "Do you have a . . . five?" If the second player answers "yes," then they will give player one the card that they asked for. Player one will then discard their two matching cards in the discard pile. If player two doesn't have the card, they will say "Go fish!" and the first player has to pick a card from the pile in the center. If the card they choose matches the one they're looking for, then they will put the pair into the discard pile. If the card is not a match, then the player must keep the card in their hand. Then their turn is over. The object of the game is to discard all of the cards in your hand. The player who runs out of cards first is the winner. You can continue playing until there's only one person with cards left.

MEMORY

Shuffle the deck. Lay the cards face down in four rows of thirteen cards each. On each player's turn, they should flip over two cards. If they match, the player will keep the cards and go again. If it's not a match, the player flips the cards back over in the exact spot they were picked up. Then the next player goes. The object is to remember where the cards are so you can collect the matches. The player with the most matches wins. You can keep playing until all the cards are gone.

SLAP JACK

Shuffle the deck. Deal the cards by giving each player a card until they're out. Going around the circle—or back and forth—each player flips the top card of their personal deck over and puts it in the center. When someone puts down a jack, the first person who slaps their hand on top of the jack gets to keep the jack and the whole pile of cards under it. Eventually some players will have no more cards to play with—those players are no longer in the game.

The last player with cards remaining is the winner. You can also change this to Slap King or Slap Queen to mix it up a little. This keeps the kids thinking!

MIRRORING

In this game, the child will copy the movements you make. Face each other in a safe, open area. Start slowly by making a movement with a hand or foot. The child should mimic the exact thing you do as you do it as if they're looking in a mirror. After a few movements, switch so that you mirror the child's movements.

MY FAVORITE THINGS

Gather some old magazines and have the child pick out about ten favorite things they find in the pages. Help them cut out the objects, then take a sheet of paper and help them make a collage by gluing the pictures onto the paper. Have some markers or crayons available if the child wants to add to the collage with some drawings.

COUNTING GAME

At this age kids are really getting into numbers and counting. Write the numbers one through ten on a card or piece of paper. Leave a blank space next to each number. Go around the house with the child (outside, too, if the weather's nice) and find something to represent each number, such as one clock, two pillows on the couch, three pens on Mommy's desk, etc., until you get to ten.

MID-ELEMENTARY SCHOOL (AGES EIGHT–TEN YEARS)

Children at this age typically spend a lot of time socializing with their friends, whether at their own house or someone else's. When babysitting, find out exactly where the child is supposed to be and at what time. If they are not home from school within fifteen minutes of the expected time, call one of the parents.

You should also make sure you know what the rules are for going to friends' houses or having friends over. Know what the child is doing and with whom at all times. The parents should tell you which friends the child is allowed to play with. Even if the child you are babysitting is with a friend, you are still responsible for them while you are being paid to watch them. If the playdate is at the house you're babysitting in, you need to be involved and supervise the children.

Make sure you always ask beforehand if a playdate is scheduled. If a parent says a child is coming over, ask if you are responsible for the other child, or if a nanny or babysitter will be coming as well. If this is the case, you and the other responsible caretaker would watch the kids together while being able to socialize with each other. In this situation you would not approach the parents about a different rate in pay.

In the case of a drop-off, one child is usually not a pay rate change, but if there are multiple children that you didn't expect to be responsible for, you should mention to the parents before the next babysitting job that your rate for three or more kids is $12, for example, instead of $10 for one or two kids. You should have these rates determined and discussed when beginning your relationship with the family so it doesn't look like you are changing your rates on the fly.

Sometimes the parents will set up a playdate that you do not have to attend. In a situation like this, your responsibility is to get the child to and from the event safely and on time. Find out who you need to drop the child off with, such as an adult contact at the playdate, party, or event. Leave the child only with that adult. Give the adult your contact information and stay nearby in case there is a problem and the child needs to be picked up early. Since you are still fully responsible for the children during this time and cannot leave the immediate area, you should still be getting paid, but it is fair to offer a reduced rate. This situation is similar to a "mother's helper" who gets paid to help watch children while the parent is still present but busy. In the playdate scenario, you are not watching the child directly, but you are still the one responsible for the child's whereabouts and wellbeing. If the child has to be sent home from the playdate for any reason, such as fighting with another child, falling down and getting hurt, or even throwing a tantrum, you need to be available to pick up the child, bring them home, and inform the parent of the situation by a call or text. The adult who is directly supervising the child should also have the contact information of the child's parents.

If nothing goes wrong, when the playdate is over, arrive on time to pick up the child and ask the adult how the event went. Be sure to find out what the child ate and if there were any problems or injuries.

Another thing that kids this age are really into is electronics. There are educational video games such as ABCmouse and ABCya, as well as popular fads, such as Minecraft and Pokémon GO, running through elementary schools like wildfire.

Some kids will have their own phones, tablets, or gaming systems but will still need permission to use them. Find out the rules about length of time and when play is allowed, and what is appropriate, just like you asked about TV watching. Also, if you're watching siblings, find out the rules about sharing and who is allowed to use what device.

Know that you are in charge, and don't be afraid to carry out the family's rules and consequences for misbehavior. But remember, children are people, too. Lay down the rules, but do your best to provide an enjoyable environment for a child. Fill the time with fun activities and the children will want to behave for you.

Here are examples of things you can try with school-age kids:

ILLUSTRATOR

Read a chapter of a book and have the children draw a picture or several pictures of the events going on as you read.

TREASURE MAP

Pick an object from the children's toys to hide. Don't choose something that is very small—you don't want it to be too hard to find. Have the child wait in their room while you hide the object. Then sit with them and draw a "treasure map" of the house. Mark the spot where the toy is hidden with an X.

Give the child the map and let them walk through the house trying to follow your directions to find the "treasure."

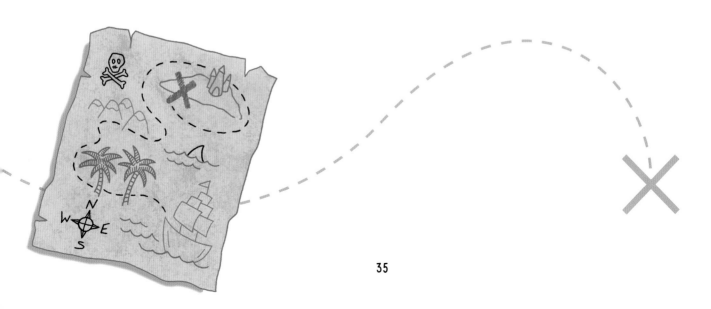

SHARING ROCK

This is more of a talking game, but it's a great one when you have several kids who love to chat. Write down the following open-ended questions on a sheet of paper, or make up your own. Find a clean, smooth stone. Sit in a circle with the kids, holding the rock. Chant "The sharing rock goes round and round, so pass it quickly through the crowd. If you're the one to hold it last, it's time for you to *share*!" while passing the rock around. Everyone says "share" loudly, and whoever has the rock at that time answers one of the questions on the below list:

- I feel happy when . . .
- One of my favorite activities is . . .
- If I won a million dollars, I would . . .
- When I grow up, I want to . . .
- One day I hope to travel to . . .
- If I were a crayon, I would be . . .
- My favorite vacation was . . .
- I get really mad when . . .
- If I had one superpower, it would be . . .

5

COMFORTING KIDS

ONCE MOM AND DAD LEAVE

No matter how happy the children you're watching generally are, there's always the chance that something will upset them and they'll need to be comforted. For younger children, this is particularly true when their parents leave the house. The absence of the child's parents may cause a lot of anxiety, and they may become angry, sad, or scared. Separation anxiety usually begins around age one. Before that, babies will generally take to babysitters or other caregivers pretty well, as long as they are given the attention and necessities they desire for comfort. As children approach one year old, they begin to realize that mom or dad is disappearing from sight but can't yet grasp that their parents will come back. This generally causes lots of tears.

The best way to deal with this is to let the parent kiss or hug the child goodbye, explain they will be back, and walk out. This should be a

consistent pattern every time the parent leaves. There's no need to hide or trick the child, which will just cause more fear and confusion when they realize Mom is gone. Let them have a quick goodbye, then take the child to a favorite activity and start to play.

Don't bring up the parents, but if a child asks about them, be direct and consistent. For example, you can say "Mommy and Daddy went out to dinner, but they will be back later. You'll see them in the morning."

Of course, this isn't the only time the child may be upset, so what can you do to help? First, stay calm. A child will pick up on your tension and anxiety and it will usually make things worse. Next, assess the situation. What is making the child cry? Are they hurt? Are they scared? If you did not see an incident occur, ask the child to tell you what hurts or why they are crying. Finally, take action to solve the problem. If it is a first-aid issue, follow the first-aid procedures in this chapter and remember to keep talking to the child the whole time using supportive and caring phrases such as "You are so brave!" If it's an emotional issue, try to put yourself in the child's shoes. Say the little girl you're babysitting dropped her doll in the sand. What would make you feel better if you were her? Pick up the doll, clean it off, and make a pretend ice pack. Always remember to offer encouraging, supportive, and caring words to the child. Never tell the child not to cry, and don't say "You're such a baby!" These words are hurtful and can make a child feel even worse. Children will usually express their emotions loudly, and cry when they are in pain or frightened, and that's a good thing. Holding emotions inside is not healthy. If the crying goes on for a while, you can say something like "It's okay, you don't have to cry. You can smile, because I'm here for you."

It's okay to say positive things, like "You've got a lot of courage," but don't say negative and accusing things, like "You're being a crybaby!"

The attention paid to a child during times of stress and anxiety is very important. You can always give them a hug and a smile to help them make it "all better."

FIRST AID

Accidents can happen at any time, no matter how cautious a babysitter you are. The important thing is that you know how to treat minor injuries when they occur. If it's a small injury or accident, such as a scrape or paper cut, you can text the parents or let them know when they get home. If it is a bigger health or safety issue, such as an allergic reaction to an insect bite or a vomiting episode, you should call the parents right away. Essentially, anything that you'd call 9-1-1 or a doctor for, the parents need to know immediately. Either way make sure you tell the parents all the details of the injury or illness before you leave the babysitting job. It may not seem like a big deal at the time, but there could be side effects or delayed reactions that show up after you leave. Below you'll find tips on the best way to deal with a variety of situations:

CUTS/SCRAPES: If a child has a small cut or scrape, the first thing you'll want to do is stop the bleeding. Use a clean cloth or gauze and apply gentle pressure to the cut. Small cuts should stop bleeding on their own. After the bleeding slows and stops, rinse the wound and then wash it gently with soap and water. Do not use any ointments, gels, or lotions unless instructed by the parents. Cover the cut with a clean bandage or gauze. Make sure the bandage stays clean and dry.

BUMPS/BRUISES: If the child has a bump or a bruise, wrap some ice cubes in a washcloth, hand towel, or two paper towels, and have the child hold the ice to the bruised area. If the injury was to the child's head, watch for vomiting, nausea, or dizziness. If you see any of these signs, call 9-1-1 and report a head injury.

BURNS: Run the burned area under cool water. Do not apply any creams or ointments. If the burn has large blisters and the skin becomes raised, call 9-1-1.

NOSEBLEEDS: Have the child sit up straight and tilt their head slightly forward. Squeeze the child's nostrils for about fifteen minutes. If bleeding does not stop after that time, or gets worse, call 9-1-1.

BUG BITES/STINGS: Apply ice, wrapped in a cloth or towel, to an itch or a painful sting. If you notice anything more than a little red mark (such as dizziness, trouble breathing, a rash, or redness spreading across the skin), call 9-1-1.

To help avoid insect bites, be sure the kids wear bug spray or other repellent when playing outside, especially if there's standing water or tall brush nearby. Insects, especially mosquitoes, can be very dangerous as they can carry and transfer diseases. As a babysitter, you should only use the spray or lotion provided by the parents. Make sure the kids don't put repellent or repellent-covered body parts into their mouths.

TICKS: When you come inside from playing, it is always important to check for ticks. Ticks can be dangerous because, like mosquitoes, they carry diseases that make people very sick. The longer a tick is on the skin, the higher the risk is for diseases, so if you see one, get it off as soon as possible.

To remove a tick, use a clean pair of tweezers and grab the part of the tick that's closest to the skin. Then in one swift motion, pull it straight out. Make sure you clean the area afterwards, and wash your hands thoroughly with soap and water. Save the tick in a plastic baggie. If the child develops any symptoms later, the tick can be tested to see what disease, if any, the child has contracted.

SPLINTERS: If the splinter is sticking out enough to grab onto, have the child sit in a comfortable place and be very still (putting on a video or TV show often helps with this). Clean a pair of tweezers with rubbing alcohol and wipe dry with a clean cloth. Under a light, grasp the piece that is sticking out and pull quickly. Wash the area and cover with a bandage. If the splinter is embedded under the skin, wash the area gently and inform the parents. Don't try to get it out yourself.

VOMITING: There are many reasons for vomiting. If the child has just eaten before running, jumping, and playing, their food may not be digested yet. See if they have a fever, dizziness, or stomach pains. If they have any of these signs of illness, call the parents and have the child lay down on their side in their bed to rest. It is important they stay on their side so they won't choke if they throw up again. Put a bucket or a big bowl by the side of the bed. If they won't stop vomiting, call 9-1-1.

CHOKING: Choking hazards include grapes, nuts, hard candy, hot dogs, popcorn, balloons, buttons, jewelry, coins, marbles, Legos, and other small toys. First talk to the child and see if they can cough, breathe, cry, or speak. If they can, encourage them to cough. This may get the item out of the child's throat. Do not attempt any first aid if the child can cough. If he can't cough or make any sound at all, begin first aid for choking. Perform the Heimlich maneuver on the child until the object comes out and they can cough.

To perform the Heimlich maneuver, stand behind the child. Wrap your arms around their waist and lean them slightly forward. Make a fist with your right hand. Position it slightly above the child's belly button. Hold your fist with your other hand and push hard into the child's tummy with a quick, upward thrust.*

STRAINS/SPRAINS: A good way to remember how to treat a sprain is by using the acronym R.I.C.E.:

---

* The section on this page regarding the Heimlich maneuver is provided as information only and is not intended to be a substitute for professional medical advice. The author and publisher are not liable for any indirect or consequential damages, including negligence, by the use of the information discussed in this publication. We encourage you to take a first-aid or safety class to learn when and how to perform the procedure correctly.

Rest! Do not put any weight or pressure on the injured area.

Ice should be applied to the injured area for twenty to thirty minutes. After this time, take off the ice and reapply it every two hours.

Compress the injury with a bandage or wrap. Don't wrap it too tightly. It should fit like a snug glove.

Elevate the injured body part above the child's heart.

It's not easy for a child to stay still very long, so while they're sitting with ice on the injury, go around the house collecting fun things for them to do, such as coloring books, puzzles, a video game, or other favorite activities.

In all cases, if the injury seems severe, or the symptoms don't go away, call 9-1-1. It's better to be overly cautious than to ignore an injury that could turn serious. And remember to tell the parents if the child has an injury, even one as small as a paper cut. You never know if a tiny cut could get infected or a bump on the head could turn out to be worse than it seems at the time.

Although these basic steps are important, the best way to soothe children of different ages varies. Here are some tips to help make your attempt a bit smoother:

INFANTS

Unlike an older child, a baby can't tell you why they're crying, so you'll have to use your senses and do some babysitting detective work to figure it out and solve the issue.

First and foremost, check over the whole child to see if there are any obvious problems, such as a diaper pin stuck in their side or a finger pinched in a toy. If there is something injuring the child, remedy it immediately and refer back to your first-aid training. As always, make sure you give the parents a full report about the injury when they get home.

You might be afraid they will be angry, but not telling them is much worse. They are most concerned about the safety and well-being of their child, so explaining what happened and how you helped will ease their anxiety and concern. Your honesty will also make them feel better about leaving their child in your care again.

If the child appears to be unharmed physically, check to see if they have a wet or dirty diaper. Even if you just changed it, a baby might go again and be uncomfortable, especially if they have diaper rash.

HOW TO CHANGE A BABY'S DIAPER

Dirty diapers can be very uncomfortable for a baby, so it's important that you check them regularly, especially when the baby wakes up from a nap. And remember, babies have sensitive skin, so be sure to wash your hands before you start changing the diaper.

When you're ready, take the baby to the changing area. If there is not a specific changing area, gather the supplies you'll need first (clean diaper, wipes or a wet rag, powder, lotion or ointment, and changing pad). If the parents do not have a changing table, set up a blanket/pad on a solid surface or the floor and lay the baby on their back.

Unlatch the stickies holding the baby's diaper on. If the baby is wearing a cloth diaper, you may have to remove the diaper cover first before unlatching. There are many different kinds of cloth diapers, and while they are not difficult to put on a baby, you may want to have the parent demonstrate how it's properly done.

While gently holding the baby's ankles together, lift up their legs and wipe their bottom with clean wipes or a wet, warm rag. For a little boy, you may want to place another wet rag or wipe over the penis so you do not get sprayed.

Wipe a girl from front to back. Be sure to get all the excrement off the baby's skin.

While you are still holding the baby's legs up, pull out the diaper in a downward motion and roll it up into a ball. Throw it into the trash or disposal container if you can do so without letting go of the baby. For a cloth diaper, you'll throw the diaper or the insert in a designated bin to be washed later.

If the parents want you to put powder, lotion, or ointment on the baby, put it on now.

Finally, slide a clean diaper under baby's bottom and place their legs back down over the elastic leg spots on the sides of the diaper. Pull up the top half over the baby's belly and attach the stickies on either side of the baby's hips. If you are changing a boy, be sure his penis is not pointed up.

When you're done, don't forget to wash your hands.

Think about the baby's feeding schedule. Is it near or past a feeding time? If the baby is crying, maybe they are just hungry and letting you know how uncomfortable an empty belly is. If they've already eaten, they may have a bubble in their tummy. Try to gently but firmly burp them. Hold them with their head over your shoulder or lay them facedown over your knees and rub and pat their back softly until they let out a burp. Keep a burp rag or hand towel on your shoulder in case they spit up. You can also sit them on your lap, and with one hand supporting their chin (not their head) gently pat their back with the other. This method takes a bit more control and practice but often helps the baby burp faster.

Another reason the baby might be crying is that they have been up for a long time, and may need a nap. Try putting them down to sleep; bounce, rock, and soothe the little one into a peaceful nap.

If the baby is not hurt, hungry, or tired, here are some other suggestions to help calm them:

RHYTHMIC MOVEMENT

Rocking, calm bouncing, and swinging are all good ways to calm a crying child. Remember, *never* shake a baby! If you are trying to calm down a crying baby in your arms and get so aggravated at the screaming that you think you might shake too hard, put the baby down in a safe place while you calm down.

RHYTHMIC SOUNDS

Newborns are used to hearing the sounds in their mother's womb—the rhythmic *thump thump thump* of her heart and the *woosh woosh* of the fluids in her body. It's not quiet in there! Sometimes the creaking of a rocking chair, ticking of a clock, or even repeating "shhh, shhh, shhh" or "wooosh, wooosh, wooosh" in a rhythm can help to calm down a baby. Try classical music or an ocean sounds CD. You may even be able to find a free app on your phone that plays relaxing ambient sounds.

TENDER TOUCH

To calm down a baby who is upset, angry, or scared, it is helpful to touch and hold them. Did you ever wonder why hugs and massages are so relaxing? Human touch causes the release of special chemicals in the baby's brain that help to relax and calm them. Hold their hand or stroke their head and cuddle that little one close to you.

SUCKING

The sucking reflex is strong in new babies. Often they try to root and may look hungry without wanting to eat. The rooting reflex is when a baby makes head motions and mouth movements like they are searching for food. They might just want to suck. If it's okay with the parents, give the baby a pacifier to suck when they seem anxious, agitated, or nervous. It's also good to suck after eating and while sleeping. Sucking on a pacifier while sleeping reduces the risk of SIDS (Sudden Infant Death Syndrome) by keeping the brain active, which ensures that the baby doesn't bury their head into a pillow as a result of falling into too deep a sleep. If the parents do not want you to give the baby a pacifier, the baby can suck on their hand or another toy, but make sure it is clean!

SWADDLING

Babies are used to a small, tight, cozy space. Out in the big wide world it is not only cooler and brighter, there is also nothing to constrict movement. This can be a bit overwhelming and frightening to a baby who puts out their arm and just hits air and more air. New babies feel more secure when they are swaddled. This means wrapping them up in a blanket a special way. The tight wrap helps to control their startle reflex as well. You might notice an infant's arms flail out when their head bends back or if something in the room scares them. This flail reflex typically disappears around two to three months of age, but in some babies it can occur up to four months, so don't be surprised if you notice it in a baby you are watching.

Swaddling not only helps with startling, it also keeps a baby warm, at a temperature they are more comfortable with. Be sure that the baby is not too warm, since they cannot regulate their own body temperature. They should only be wearing very light clothing or just a diaper, and don't swaddle if the room is too warm.

Make sure you ease the transition from one activity to another and avoid overstimulating the baby with too many sounds, sights, or smells. They are so little, it is easy for them to become overwhelmed!

HOW TO SWADDLE

Some parents may ask you to swaddle their newborn. Swaddling a baby means wrapping a blanket around their body tightly in order to keep them secure. Some parents may not want this, however, so make sure you check in with your clients before swaddling their baby.

Get a baby blanket that is made from cotton or a similar material that won't easily stretch out.

Place the blanket on a firm, safe surface with the top corner pointing up, like a diamond. Fold that top corner down.

Next, put the baby on their back on to the blanket. That top fold should be right under their little neck.

It should now look like the baby is lying on a diamond with no top point. There will be a point by their right arm, a point by their left, and a bottom point under their feet.

Take the corner that's near the baby's right arm and pull it across their body.

Tuck that corner under their left arm and around under their back.

Now take the bottom point. Pull it up over their tummy and gently tuck it under the right side of the baby's neck and head.

Now you have one more point left, near the baby's left arm. Take the last point and pull it across their body to the right. Tuck it under their back on their right side. If you have enough blanket, pull it across their back and over to their left side.

Hold the little bundle close and rock them gently, while singing, talking, or making shushing sounds.

If a baby is over eight weeks old, make sure it is okay with the parents to try swaddling. For older babies, it's better to keep the legs loose in the wrap.

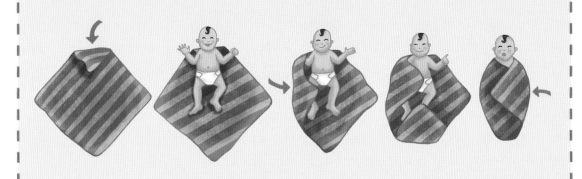

TODDLERS

Between twelve and twenty-four months (one to two years) toddlers often have problems controlling their feelings and emotions. They tend to overexpress things and become very dramatic. That's totally normal for this age.

Toddlers often have comfort objects like a teddy bear, doll, or blanket. When they are crying or upset, bring them this special object and ask the child to give it a hug. These special objects can help them self-soothe and self-calm when upset.

Music can also help a toddler forget they are angry. Find a kids' CD, digital station on your phone, or a fun and appropriate radio station that you can dance to. Music from movies the kids like is always a good way to get them singing and dancing. Play the music in the background and ask the child if they want to dance. If you get an angry or pouty "no," start to dance yourself. This works especially well if the child has a favorite song or CD. Another thing you can do is start singing along to the music. If the child is still resistant, you can pretend to get the words wrong and see if they start singing it right to correct you. It's okay to be silly! Sometimes a sad child needs a laugh more than they know. Act like a clown for them! Put a stuffed animal on your head or make funny faces. Bringing the child into the action can help as well. Give them a stuffed animal to put on their own head and ask if they can balance it up there. Funny things distract the child from tears or sad thoughts.

PRESCHOOL-AGE KIDS

By this age, children are old enough to understand why they are angry or sad and can clearly express it. They are also more conversational. Here are some good ways to get the child talking about why they are upset (or to comfort them if they don't want to talk):

- Ask the child why they are sad and try to talk about their feelings.
- Take out some paper and crayons. Ask them to draw a picture about how they are feeling.
- Take out some dolls or action figures. Ask if the child would like to tell their dolls about the angry or sad feelings. You can even begin a make-believe play with the dolls to help the child express their feelings. Use the dolls to repeat what happened in real life. Start the scenario yourself and see if the child picks up playing with you.

Playing make-believe is a fantastic way for a child to work out anger, especially when they do not feel like talking or have problems saying what they feel.

- Ask if the child wants a hug.
- Ask if the child would like to hug their favorite doll or toy.
- Change the subject and introduce something fun to do, like "Hey! Want to go outside and play on your swing set?" or "Meghan, can you show me how this bomerangadoozle works?"
- Remember, don't yell at an angry child—raising your voice only makes the child raise their own voice in competition.

SCHOOL-AGE KIDS

Comforting an older child generally involves discussion. Talk to them about what's making them sad and what they want to do. Let them know that they don't have to talk, but you are there to listen if they want to. Talk about your own experiences when you were younger and had a babysitter, or what you remember from your own life about the situation that is upsetting them. Personal experiences and reflections can help you reach out to them. You can also try giving them some alone time in their room to write, play video games, read, watch TV, or draw.

Sometimes an older child is upset about something and doesn't want to discuss it. That's okay. As long as they are being safe, find something they like to do and let them take their own time to come out of their shell.

And remember, even older kids need a hug sometimes! Make sure they know they are important and that you are there if they need you.

FIGHTING

DEALING WITH A FEUD

Children will fight with each other—it's a fact of life. Often you'll run into a spell of anger when you're babysitting. It's important to address this in the correct way. Remember to discuss discipline with the parents. As with the rest of your time babysitting, it's essential to set limits, be consistent, and mirror healthy behavior.

When children get angry or become fussy and you can't figure out why, remember that they may be tired, bored, or hungry. Try discussing the problem to figure out why they are upset. If that doesn't work, here are some useful tips to make the fighting stop:

TODDLERS

When a toddler gets in a fight with another child, they could be making a statement that they need your acknowledgment. Sharing simple exercises to build a relationship with the child you are babysitting is a good step in positive care. Activities such as reading together, making dinner together, and pointing out different objects on a walk around the block are simple but effective bonding and learning experiences that help to minimize anxiety, stress, and anger in young children. Believe it or not, stress affects even little kids, and can make a huge difference in their attitudes and how quick they are to argue. Relaxing activities, talking, and sharing help ease the stress that can lead to anger and fighting, and can help prevent a lot of arguments before they happen.

If the toddler starts fighting with another child—whether it be a friend or a sibling—try introducing a relaxing activity. It can really help calm down the situation! It's perfectly normal for kids to fight, and luckily, the fights are usually short. Toddlers are very "me" focused, so a good way to break up a toddler fight is to start talking about the child's likes and interests and what they are good at. "Xavier, wow, look—it's a dinosaur! Don't you love dinosaurs? I'll bet this is a T. rex, or is it a Triceratops?" Get them talking about what they can control.

When a young child refuses to share, grabs a toy away from their friend or sibling, or yells at or hits another child, try asking them what they think of their own behavior. Instead of reprimanding them, ask, "Patrick, do you think that makes Kai feel happy or sad?" Also ask, "So what do you think will happen now?" Using a questioning, positive approach makes kids feel understood.

PRESCHOOLERS

At this age arguments and tantrums may come from a variety of situations. Preschool children often get angry about sharing toys—especially around babysitters who may act differently than parents. With two or three children, toys become prizes, and friends or siblings will fight over something that may seem interesting one moment and boring the next.

Speak to the child who had the toy first. Set a time limit for play and encourage sharing after that time limit. "You can play with this for fifteen minutes, and then Abby gets a turn for fifteen minutes." Time is a confusing concept at this age, but setting a timer is a good and direct way to be fair and to make a point. A timer on a kitchen stove, microwave, or cell phone works the best, so they can hear the "ding" when the time's up. Allow the child to pass on the toy after the limit is up. If they do not obey, take the toy away.

Find another toy in the meantime to replace the desire for the one the child wants. Pick out something in the room that looks fascinating and make a big deal about it. "Wow, Abby, look at this pony! While Kayla has the castle, you can play with this pretty pony with the rainbow hair." Encourage the child to play, and you can even play along to make it more interesting! "Look, I can brush her hair. Wow—it gets so shiny when you brush it. Do you want to try?" Be careful, though. You don't want to make the new toy so fabulous that the children begin fighting over that one instead.

If this doesn't work, you may find that the best solution is to take away the item from both kids. This especially works with the younger ones, such as four- and five-year-olds fighting over a toy truck. Let them both pick out another toy and put the truck in a place where they can see it but not reach it, such as on top of the refrigerator. This way if they start to fight over another toy, you can look up at the truck with a look that warns them that if they don't stop fighting, their other toys could end up on top of the fridge.

SCHOOL-AGE KIDS

Older kids know the rules. Start by letting them know that. Generally, fighting is born from an activity that is not allowed, such as hitting. Tell the children you might take something away from them if they don't stop their misbehavior. For example, "No dessert if you don't stop hitting your sister."

You can also try the guilt tactic with older children. "Ava, you've been so good all day, what's going on now? Are you not feeling well?" If you act surprised and disappointed by their bad behavior, older children will often stop fighting so as not to disappoint you or their parents.

Just as with younger kids, introducing a new activity can sometimes distract the kids from fighting and focus them on something else in a positive way. Think of something you can do that will take their attention in a whole new direction, such as going for a walk, watching a movie, playing a video game, or starting a craft project. If they were already doing an activity, stop that activity until they are done fighting.

SIBLING RIVALRY

With sibling rivalry, you can often think of funny games to help the siblings bond. When a little tension arises, try pulling out a mirror and making them both stare at each other in it. Kids will often make silly faces and eventually end up laughing at each other and at themselves, forgetting whatever started their silly argument in the first place.

Remember that it's not always the older child's fault. Don't be quick to judge or blame. If you didn't see the incident that started the fighting, listen to both sides of the story, and then choose new activities for both children.

If it gets violent, be sure to separate fighting kids! You don't want anyone to get hurt. They'll probably tell you "He started it!" Keep focused on the fact that it's not who started it, it's how we are going to end it. Encourage talk about the solution, not the problem. "Let's have a happy ending. Who is going to help me end the fight and move on to something fun!" If they're both still arguing, they need to be separated until they calm down and cool off. Try moving the fighting kids to different areas to play with different toys.

A child will often feel or say that their brother or sister is not as good as they are. When this happens it is important to sit both children down and focus on the good things each child possesses. Ask both of them to name three things that are good about themselves, and then three things that are good about their sibling. You can even make it into an art project—write the special qualities on construction paper or draw pictures to illustrate those qualities.

TEMPER TANTRUMS

There are many reasons that a child will turn from a sweet, happy, bouncy angel to a screaming little terror, and there's usually no way to predict it. Don't blame yourself or even the parents—it happens. A child may throw a tantrum if you tell them they cannot have a cookie until after dinner when they insist they want it "NOW!" Or maybe you decide it's too cold to go outside without a coat and the child simply will not wear one. Remember to stay calm. You're the big person, and they're the little person. Take a deep breath and let it out slowly. Speak in a calm voice. Yelling will only aggravate the situation even more when the child follows your lead and starts yelling back. The other magical thing about speaking quietly is that even though the child is throwing a fit, they probably want to know what you're saying, so they'll have to be quiet to hear you, if only for a moment. That moment can stop the escalation of a tantrum.

Generally, you'll find kids two to five years old going through these little fits, often whining, kicking, and screaming. When children get older, you can reason with them a little better and explain why the rule has been set. You may have to approach this discussion after the tantrum, though, as anger tends to block out what they don't want to hear. With an older child you can even talk about why they were angry after the emotion has passed. Don't try to ask questions during a fit, because they cannot think or care about the "why" in the middle of a tantrum. It's best to talk things through afterward to try and find ways to prevent a similar incident from happening again.

So what are they throwing a tantrum about? Think about something they might want or something they want to do and focus on it. You can turn an angry situation into a happy one. For example, "You can play on the jungle gym if we go outside, but you have to wear your coat to play on the jungle gym." Or "You can have the candy after dinner, but you must eat a healthy dinner before you can have the candy." Mention what they want several times in the sentence so they know you are addressing the situation. Not only will this get their attention, it will show them you really do care about the things that matter to them. Just be sure you follow through with your promise!

If a child still won't listen to you, it might help for you to start playing with something they love to do. For example, take out the crayons, sit down at the table, and start coloring. You don't even have to ask the child to join you. As a matter of fact, it often works better if you don't. The child will probably come up to you to see what you're doing and want to join you. Be nice, even if the child was mean to you. Children speak what's on their minds and don't mean to hurt with what they say. They may hate you one second and love you the next. Things said in a temper tantrum may be hateful, but remember not to take it personally.

PUNISHMENT

Preschool, elementary, and middle school children have the ability to know right from wrong. Babies do not. Do not try to punish a baby for doing something you may consider "wrong" or "bad." A baby will not understand. It is okay to teach them what they cannot do, but do not punish them for doing it. For example, if a six-month-old is pulling on a cord in the living room, take it away from them and tell them "No," or "You will get hurt," and hide the cord so they can't get to it again. Then redirect their attention to something else. They probably just think it's a toy, so give them a toy they can play with.

Discuss with the parents what their form of punishment is for their child or children. There are many different parenting styles so be sure you understand what these kids are used to. Some parents have a time-out chair or put the kids in "thinking time" when they do something wrong. A good rule for this is to let the child sit for as long as their age, (so a three-year-old would be in the chair for three minutes). After the time is up, make sure you talk about what they did wrong and give a solution or example for what to do next time that is a better choice.

Another common punishment is removing something that they love to play with. This punishment is better if it "fits the crime," so to speak. So if they are fighting with a sibling over the TV show they want to watch, a good punishment would be no TV for either child the rest of the day.

Some children use the "star chart" system when they get points or stars for doing something good. If they misbehave, you might be able to remove a star from their chart that must be earned back by a good deed or a chore. This is a great way for them to visually understand the consequences of their actions.

Make sure that the punishment is approved by the parents. For example, don't say you will take them out of swim class or that they can't go to a birthday party next week if they don't stop fighting. Not only is this not your place to makes these decisions, it is also out of your hands to enforce it. The punishment must be appropriate, not harmful or unsafe. Don't tell them they cannot have dinner if they refuse to do homework. It is important as a babysitter not to use corporal punishment or spanking. If a child is making you that angry, you need to take a breath—step away, and count to ten before facing them again. It is never okay to hit.

ACTIVITIES AND CRAFTS

HAVE FUN!

Babysitting isn't just about supervising the children so they are not alone. It is also about coming up with fun activities to do. A babysitter should be able to get on the kids' level and be directly involved with activities, crafts, playtime, and fun.

When planning crafts and activities with babies, keep in mind that infants put everything in their mouths! Wash toys if they become dirty and be sure they cannot be swallowed. As a general rule, if it's small enough to fit in a toilet paper roll, it's too small for a child under three. Keep such toys or art materials away from babies and look for something safer to play with. Some easy activities include simple arts and crafts, backyard play, reading, going for a walk, and playing make-believe. Parents will be happy

that their kids are involved with activities that will help them learn and grow, and kids will be thrilled to try new games!

As you're planning your activities, remember, do not let young children play with anything that has a cord, long string, or sharp ends, like the string hanging from the mini-blinds or that barbecue fork in the kitchen drawer. If you have a battery-operated toy, do not put it in the bathtub or kiddie pool (unless it is designed to go there and has been manufactured for water safety). As a general rule, don't get anything wet that is not a bath toy, unless it has been pointed out by the parents as okay to use.

IS IT OKAY TO PLAY WITH MAKE-BELIEVE GUNS?

Ask parents if they allow their children to play with make-believe guns. Lots of kids like to pretend they're cowboys or police officers, so this may come up. If it's okay with parents, be sure that the child is playing with a make-believe gun in a safe manner. Both toys and imaginary guns should be pointed away from people at all times. The make-believe play should be centered on a safe, non-violent, gun-toting person, like a cowboy shooting at a target or a space hero shooting at an alien to protect the ship.

If the children are not allowed to use guns and you see one of them using a hand or another toy as a gun, redirect the activity. Pretend it is a fire hose and say "Wow! Keep shooting that water on the fire. It's doing a great job to put it out!" Or maybe it's a flashlight and you can say "Melissa! That's great! Aim that flashlight in the woods over by that chair so Becky can find her way home!" Use your imagination to change the focus of their game.

Chapter 4 contains a list of age-appropriate activities (page 25). Below are more activities and crafts for kids of all ages. As you come up with additional ideas or hear about something that the kids enjoy, write them down and keep them handy.

ANIMAL HUNT

Bring a notebook on a walk or into the backyard and have the children write down or draw every different species they see. If you want, you can make the hunt more specific and just look for a certain kind of creature, like bugs or birds.

NAME THAT TUNE

Play just a tiny bit of a song and ask the child to guess what song it is. Be sure to use songs the children will be familiar with.

SCAVENGER HUNT

Make a list of silly things the children have to find and check off or put a gold star sticker on the paper every time they find one. This could be indoors ("Find a blond-haired doll or a green block.") or outdoors ("Find a pinecone or a gray pebble."). If you are babysitting more than one child, it might be fun for them to create their own scavenger hunt lists and then swap.

MUSICAL OBJECTS

Set out things to sit on in a wide-open space, like outdoors or the playroom. These can be a baby blanket, a coloring book, etc. Play this just like musical chairs. You play music, and when the music stops, yell out the name of one item on the floor. The child must quickly find and sit on that object. If they don't find it, take it away, until all the items are gone.

ARACTS AND CRAFTS

Kids of all ages love arts and crafts. Children will usually have their own craft supplies, but if you're unsure about what they have or if you have a specific project in mind, you may want to create a babysitting bag full of your own supplies. This not only allows you to control what the kids play with, but parents will be impressed that you're so prepared.

Here are some ideas about what to put into your babysitting bag:

- chalk
- construction paper
- crayons

- empty egg cartons
- feathers, buttons, and other things to glue onto paper (for kids over three)
- fingerpaints
- glitter
- handful of cereal pieces, such as toasted Os or corn puff balls
- kid-safe glue
- kid-safe paint
- kid-safe scissors (with rounded tips)
- old shirts for smocks
- old sponges that are clean and dry
- pipe cleaners
- small pieces of cut felt or material
- toilet paper tubes
- watercolor paint

Use your imagination. All sorts of weird objects can become craft supplies. Kids will know what to do with them, so lay out the materials and let them get to work. Below are some great art projects in case the kids need direction. If the kids are too young to do these projects on their own, you will need to help them, especially with cutting. Always put down newspaper in the work area for easy cleanup.

FISH

Get a paper plate and cut a wedge out of the left side—like a pizza slice. Glue or tape the wedge, point in, on the right side as a tail. The space you cut out is the mouth of the fish. Draw an eye on the fish and let the child decorate it with crayons or markers, drawing fins and scales. You can even punch a hole in the top and hang it!

HANDPRINT FLOWERS

Put a little bit of kid-safe paint on a paper plate. If the child isn't old enough to do so alone, place their hand in the paint and cover their palm with paint. Lift up the little hand and help the child press it down onto a piece of construction paper (toward the top of the paper). Repeat this step

three or four times in a row so that the top of the paper is covered in palm prints. While the paint is drying, have the child wash their hands. When the paper is dry, allow the child to draw stems and leaves below the hands as if the hands were flowers.

VEGGIE PRINTS

Ask the parents if you can use a squash, apple, potato, or other firm piece of food for an art project. Put a little bit of kid-safe paint on a paper plate. Cut the veggie in half or thirds, making a good size to hold in your hand. Have the child dip the flat side of the vegetable into the paint, then press it onto a piece of construction paper to make a print, like a stamp. Make as many prints as you want on the sheet of paper. If you have a long roll of white paper, or even a paper bag, this is a fun way to make your own wrapping paper.

WHIPPED CREAM PAINTING

Squirt a little bit of whipped cream onto a paper plate. Put one drop of food coloring on the cream and allow the child to squish it up with their hands. Have paper ready so they can make a design, handprint, or squiggles with their fingers.

INSTRUMENTS

Get some empty bottles of different sizes. You may want to ask the parents if they have a plastic water or soda bottle in the recycling bin. Peel off the labels and clean the bottles out. While they are drying, collect a bunch of little noise-making items, such as macaroni noodles, buttons, or rice. You won't need more than a handful. Help the child drop the items into the bottles. Screw the lid back on and allow the child to color on the side of the bottles with crayons. When you're done, turn on some music and shake them to the beat!

TOUCH-AND-FEEL BOOK

One fun activity is creating a touch-and-feel book. You will need a variety of different textured materials such as cotton balls, scraps of velvet fabric, aluminum foil, sandpaper, or dried leaves. You'll also need construction paper, crayons, scissors, and a stapler to make the book. Set out paper and help the child glue different textures onto different pages. Let the pages dry and then staple them together. Write a descriptive word such as "rough," "smooth," or "shiny" on each page and encourage the child to feel the objects and talk about what they notice.

When you're done, add a blank sheet on the cover. If the child can write their name, write "_____'s Book" and have them fill it in. If they are too young, hold their hand and write the letters with them.

MY NAME
Write the child's name in big block or bubble letters on a sheet of paper. For each letter, let the child choose something they like or an activity they like to do, then use crayons or markers to color in and design the letter based upon the activity they choose. For example, *KYLIE*: *K* = Kites, *Y* = Yellow, *L* = Lions, *I* = Ice Cream, *E* = Elephants.

DRAWING WITH CHILDREN

Toddlers and preschool kids often draw pictures that seem very clear and obvious to them. However, it might look like a scribble or a bunch of lines to an adult. It can hurt their feelings if they show you a picture of a squiggle that they are proud of and you ask them what it is. Instead, ask them to tell you about the picture. This will allow them to explain what it is without being insulted that you couldn't identify the squiggly line as their best friend or their pet.

LETTER HOLDER
Get two paper plates and cut one in half. Staple the plates together. The half plate will become a pouch to put notes or letters in. Staple or tape a string across the top of the whole plate so the child can hang the letter holder on a doorknob. Write "My Notes" in big letters across the pouch and have them decorate the holder with crayons, markers, stickers, or stamps. When the letter holder is done, the child's siblings or parents can leave notes in it for them—just like their own mailbox.

SOCK PUPPETS
Get a few old socks, stickers, and markers. Put a sock over your hand. When you open and close your hand, you can turn it into a puppet! The thumb is the bottom of the mouth and the four fingers are the top. The tops of your fingers and

knuckles are the rest of the face. Put stickers on the sock for features like the eyes, nose, and mouth. You can even make silly animals; draw whiskers to make a cat or a big, round nose for a pig. Once you have made a few, have a puppet show or play a make-believe game with your puppets. Unless you've brought your own socks, be sure to ask the parents before you draw anything on the socks.

WHAT'S THAT CLOUD?

You know how you can look up in the clouds and use your imagination to find pictures and objects? Well you can do that on paper, too! Take a crayon, marker, or pen and draw a bunch of twisted, twirly, loopy, scribbly lines on a sheet of paper. Then sit with the child you are babysitting and see if the two of you can find things together! You can even use other colors to pick out, color in, or expand upon the shapes you find!

PUZZLES

Find an old magazine, a pencil, glue or a glue stick, scissors, and a piece of cardboard. Have the child pick out a picture and glue it onto the cardboard. Then let them draw (or help them draw) odd-shaped lines like puzzle pieces across the picture with a pencil. Be sure you don't put too many lines because you will want fairly large pieces. Cut or have the child cut on the lines to make the pieces separate. Mix them up and have the child put them together again like a puzzle!

SEASONAL CREATIONS

Seasonal crafts are fun to make, too. Here are some fun and easy projects:

AUTUMN LEAVES

Go on a leaf hunt in the backyard! Pick up different colored leaves and glue them onto construction paper. You can even let the child color and glitter the leaves. This is good for ages two and up—just watch that the little ones don't eat the leaves.

If you don't have any fallen leaves to pick up, you can make your own. Pick out red, brown, and yellow crayons. Tape the three crayons together to make one fat crayon, and then let the child scribble on a sheet of paper with the tri-colored crayon. This will make a wonderful mixture of fall colors. When the child is done, fold the paper into quarters and cut out the shape of a leaf.

TURKEY HAND

Trace the child's hand onto a sheet of white paper and round off the bottom by drawing a line from the bottom of the thumb to the bottom of the pinkie. This is going to be a turkey! Under this line, draw two turkey legs. The child's thumb is the head. Put a little eye in the top and a squiggly red wattle under the chin. The four fingers are the turkey's feathers. Let the child color the turkey's head and body. Add a wing in the center. Pick out different colors for the feathers and color each finger-feather in.

WINTER SNOWFLAKES

Cut or help the child cut snowflake shapes out of coffee filters. After they are cut, help the kid glue them onto dark-blue construction paper. The glue will squish through the holes as they spread it with their fingers and can be sprinkled with clear and/or silver glitter. The snowflakes make great holiday cards that kids can share with their friends. This project is good for Valentine's Day, too. Just use red paper and cut out hearts instead of snowflakes.

If snow doesn't fall in your part of the country, you can take this opportunity to talk to the child about snow.

REINDEER

Trace the child's foot onto a dark-brown piece of construction paper and their hands onto a piece of light-brown construction paper or a paper bag. Cut out the foot (this is the head) and hands (these are the antlers). Glue the antlers on the top of the head. Decorate with a big red nose, eyes, and a mouth.

SPRING FLOWERS

Put water in two or three glasses. In each glass, put one drop of food coloring. Fold a coffee filter in half, and then again in half, and hand it to the child. Let them dip a corner of the filter into each color. Place the wet filter on a plate or foil to dry. When it is dry, open the coffee filter. Pinch and twist the center of the filter. Attach a green pipe cleaner by wrapping the end of the pipe cleaner around the piece you have pinched, which should be sticking out.

PAPER BUGS

Let the child color a paper plate with crayons. From construction paper, cut out circles that will be used for spots, two strips that will be used for antennae, and two oval shapes that will be used for wings. After the child colors the body, help them glue the body parts on.

SUMMER SEASHORE ART

For this craft, you'll need to bring some sand. Encourage the child to draw a picture of the beach on a piece of paper or a plate. When the drawing is complete, put glue over the sections of the picture that will have sand. Help the child shake sand onto the picture and then set it aside to dry. When the picture is dry, invite them to touch and feel the sand art!

SUMMERTIME MOBILE

Get a hanger, some yarn or string, construction paper, and magazines. Give the magazines to the child and let them find pictures that remind them of summertime, like a beach ball, a sun, or someone on a skateboard. Help the child cut out the pictures and glue them onto the construction paper. Then cut around each picture, leaving a small border of paper. Punch a hole in the top of each one and tie a six-inch piece of string through each hole. Tie the pictures onto the hanger by their strings. On a nice, breezy day, you can take the mobile outside and see how the wind blows the summer objects around.

KITCHEN PROJECTS

If you prefer projects that don't use the typical arts and crafts supplies, try some of the activities listed on the following pages. Before you begin these activities, ask for permission to "cook" in the kitchen. It's a good idea to show the parents what you plan to make before you begin. Remember, keep the kids *away* from the stove. You will also want to ask if they have the ingredients you need and if it's okay to use them. You might have to bring your own, so it's good to know beforehand what is available to you.

MAKE YOUR OWN PLAYDOUGH

YOU NEED:

- 1 cup flour
- ½ cup salt
- 1 package unsweetened powdered drink mix
- 1 tbsp oil
- 1 cup boiling water

DIRECTIONS:

1. Mix the flour, salt, and drink mix together in a bowl.
2. Add the oil and the boiling water.
3. Stir the mixture until it is well blended. Remove the mixture from the bowl and knead it until it forms a soft dough that you can play with.
4. Let the kids build all kinds of fun objects with the dough.

GELATIN SHAPES

YOU NEED:

- 3 envelopes unflavored gelatin
- ¾ cup boiling water
- 3 12-oz. cans of frozen apple, orange, grape, or other juice concentrate

DIRECTIONS:

1. This is a good one to start when you first get to the house so it will have time to settle. Dissolve the gelatin in the boiling water, and then separate it into three different bowls, one for each juice flavor.
2. Add one different can of juice to each different bowl of gelatin, and stir until mixed. When you add the frozen juice to the bowl of gelatin, it will melt quickly since the water will still be warm. Stir it up until it's completely melted. This is something the kids can help with.
3. Next, pour the gelatin-juice mixture into three lightly greased pans (one for each juice flavor) and chill in the refrigerator for several hours. When the gelatin is firm, give the kids cookie cutters and let them cut out shapes. They'll have fun playing with their food and will enjoy sampling the different tastes.

PEANUT BUTTER PLAYDOUGH

YOU NEED:

- 2 cups peanut butter
- 2 cups powdered milk
- 1 cup honey or corn syrup

DIRECTIONS:

1. Mix all of the ingredients together in a bowl until it forms dough.
2. Give the child a cookie sheet or plastic tray, and a small ball of dough. Let them smash and mold it and try a little nibble! It's fun to create shapes with, and it's delicious!

SAND JARS

YOU NEED:

- Sand
- Food coloring
- Clear sealable jars
- Plastic cups

DIRECTIONS:

1. Pour sand into a few plastic cups.
2. Let the kids mix in food coloring to add color to the sand (you may want to add a little water to help disperse the color).
3. When the sand is dry, pour it into a clear jar (an old tomato-sauce jar works well), layering the colors any way they want.
4. When the jar is full, put on the lid and let the kids display their art in their room.

BUBBLE TIME

YOU NEED:

- 1 cup water
- ⅓ cup dish soap
- 2 tbsp light corn syrup

DIRECTIONS:

1. Mix all the ingredients together in a large bowl.
2. Use a stretched-open wire hanger to make a bubble wand that you can blow through or swoosh through the air.
3. You can also use the children's beach or bath toys to make bubbles. Look for a plastic toy that has a hole in it. Dip the toy into the bowl, covering the hole completely with the bubble liquid, then lift the toy out and gently swing it or blow into it to make bubbles!

SOLID OR LIQUID?

YOU NEED:

- 1½ cups water
- Food coloring
- 2 cups cornstarch
- Wax paper

DIRECTIONS:

1. In a large bowl, slowly mix the water and a few drops of food coloring into the cornstarch.
2. When it is mixed, let the kids play with the weird substance over a sheet of wax paper. Is it solid or liquid? Actually, it's both at the same time!

WRAP IT UP

YOU NEED:

- ½ cup water
- 1 tsp dish soap
- Food coloring
- Plastic cup
- Baking sheet
- Plastic drinking straw
- White drawing paper
- Markers

DIRECTIONS:

1. Mix water, soap, and a few drops of food coloring in a plastic cup, then place the plastic cup on a baking sheet.

2. Put the straw in the cup and blow bubbles through the straw until they spill all over the baking sheet. The kids can help with this part, but make sure they only blow *out* through the straw so that they do not swallow any soap.

3. Remove the cup and place a piece of paper on top of the bubbles. Lift the paper off gently. The colored bubbles will create a light design on the paper.

4. Let it dry and then the child can draw on it. This is a fun project for making stationary or book covers.

8

TIME TO EAT

YUMMY!

If you are babysitting over a mealtime, parents will generally have a plan. It will likely be something simple, such as ordering pizza, making macaroni and cheese from a box, or heating up leftovers. Some parents will leave a detailed list of what their kids can and can't eat. It's important to find out if any of the children have special food or diet restrictions, even if you get approval from the parents to use any food in the house. One child may be lactose intolerant but the milk in the fridge is fine for their sister. If there are severe allergies, like peanuts or pepper, be sure that all the food you prepare is in a clean and separated area from any other food. If a child is gluten-free, make sure to avoid foods with gluten like wheat bread or pasta.

Parents may make food restriction decisions that are not based on allergies, such as no junk food or sugar. These choices are important to

acknowledge and respect just as you respect the allergy-related dietary constraints. If the parents would like you to cook something, make sure before they leave that they've provided all the ingredients and the instructions. If you feel something is beyond your skill level, just let the parents know. Besides allergies, families may have specific food choices based on cultural or religious beliefs. Respect cultural differences by learning about and complying with these traditions when you're in their home. This could include saying prayers before meals or not eating pork or beef.

Most kids can eat on their own, but babies are another story. If you have to feed a baby, first find out if the baby is on a schedule or eats on-demand. Follow the schedule closely, or in the case of demand feeding (many breastfeeding babies are on-demand), be sure to have a bottle ready for when the baby gets fussy. If the parents do not have pre-prepared bottles for you to use, prepare one while the baby is in a good mood. That way, when it's time for feeding or when they're cranky, you can save the trouble and hassle of preparation and just heat it up. Ask the parents when the best time is to feed them. Babies have tiny stomachs, so don't worry if they don't eat a lot in one sitting. They eat a little at each feeding and need to be fed pretty frequently.

SANITATION

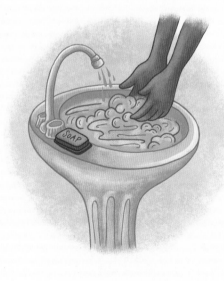

Anytime you are working with food, remember to wash your hands. The children should wash their hands, too. In order to make sure their hands are fully clean, the child should wash for twenty seconds. Try singing "The Alphabet Song," "Twinkle, Twinkle, Little Star," or "Mary Had a Little Lamb" to time the hand-washing process.

If you are working with anything uncooked—such as chicken breasts—be sure to wipe all surfaces with a sanitized wipe or soap and warm water. Do not let anything that touched the uncooked food (such as a spoon) touch anything else. If it does, put it in the sink and wash it.

Remember to *wash your hands* before handling the bottle. Find out how the parents want you to warm the bottles. They might have an appliance called a bottle warmer that heats up the milk or formula. Typically, heating a pot of water to a simmer and then placing the sealed bottle of milk or formula in the pot is the best way to warm a bottle. Microwaves can heat unevenly, overcook formula and breast milk, and kill important nutrients.

To check the temperature of the bottle, shake it to distribute the heat evenly and then squirt a bit of milk onto the inside of your wrist or the inside of your elbow (you may need to squeeze the nipple a bit). These are the most sensitive parts of your body and will be the best judge of the temperature. If it feels cool on your skin, place it back in the hot water or bottle warmer for a few minutes and check it again. If it stings your skin, the bottle is too warm. Put it in the refrigerator for a few minutes then check it again. It should never feel hot on your skin. You want it to feel lukewarm and comfortable. Some parents have a heat-strip that you stick on the side of the bottle to check the temperature. If you have questions about how to use any baby care items at all, make sure you ask the parents.

When you are ready to feed the baby, hold them securely in your lap with one arm around them and their head resting by your elbow. The rooting reflex is important in getting a baby to eat. This reflex is an automatic reaction newborn babies have; if something lightly brushes their cheeks, it makes them turn their heads and start sucking. To start the feeding, brush a finger across the baby's cheek closest to your body. The baby should turn their face toward you and their lips should part slightly.

Gently push the nipple of the bottle into the baby's open mouth, keeping their head and upper body raised at a slight angle so that it's easier for the baby to swallow. Tip the end of the bottle up as you're feeding so that the baby doesn't swallow air with breast milk or formula.

Once you have finished feeding the baby, remember to burp them. Babies will take in some air while drinking a bottle and burping helps to get rid of this air so they don't have gas or tummy cramps.

Use soft, gentle pats on the baby's back. You can hold the baby over your shoulder or across your legs with their tummy on your lap. Remember that the baby might spit up, so keep a burp cloth handy or place one under their chin.

Older kids may be easier to feed, but they tend to be picky. If this happens, try to remind them that snacks and mealtime can be fun, especially when you prepare the food together. There is a list of fun recipes you can try out on page 71. Before you make any of these, be sure to get the parents' permission to use the kitchen appliances. When babysitting little ones, remember not to give small, solid foods such as hard candies, nuts, and popcorn to children under the age of three. Foods like grapes, mini tomatoes, and hot dogs should be squished or diced into very small pieces. These foods can get lodged in young children's throats and cause choking.

As you find more recipes, write them down and keep them somewhere you can easily find them or store them in your phone under "babysitting recipes."

STOVE SAFETY

If the parents have given you permission to use the stove, keep handles of pots and pans turned away from the front of the stove so they don't stick out over the edge and cannot be grabbed by little hands and knocked over.

Don't let the children near the oven as you are putting food in, or taking it out. Make sure they are not behind you where you can trip over them with a hot pan in your hand.

BREAKFAST

These meals aren't limited to the morning, though—you can eat them anytime!

FRUIT CREPE
(VEGETARIAN)

MAKES 4 CREPES
YOU NEED:

- 1 cup all-purpose flour
- 2 eggs
- ½ cup milk
- ½ cup water
- Dash of salt
- 2 tbsp oil or butter

- Plain or vanilla yogurt
- About ½ cup diced fruit (strawberries, bananas, peaches, blueberries, etc.)
- 1 tbsp brown sugar

DIRECTIONS:

1. In a mixing bowl, combine the flour, eggs, milk, water, and salt. Beat with a fork or whisk to combine. The child can do this while you heat the oil in a pan on low to medium heat.

2. When the oil starts to sizzle, pour ¼ cup of the mixture in the pan, swirling the pan slightly to spread the mixture into a thin layer, and cook until the edges are light brown.

3. With a spatula, gently flip over. Keep the kids away from the stove for this in case there is a hot splatter of oil.

4. Once the other side is lightly browned, remove it from the pan and place it on a plate. Let the child spoon some yogurt and fruit on top. Sprinkle with brown sugar and enjoy!

HOLEY EGG!
(VEGETARIAN)

MAKES 2 SERVINGS

YOU NEED:

- A small drinking glass or round cookie cutter
- 2 slices bread
- 2 tbsp butter
- 2 eggs
- 2 slices American cheese

DIRECTIONS:

1. With the cookie cutter or drinking glass, cut out a hole in the center of each bread slice. The child can help with this part.

2. Melt butter in a pan large enough to hold both slices of bread over low heat. When melted, place the bread in the pan.

3. Next, crack open one egg and drop it into the hole in one slice of bread. Repeat for the second slice.

4. Cook the eggs until they are opaque for sunny-side up. You can flip the egg and bread over for a more fully cooked egg if you wish.

5. Once the eggs are cooked, put a slice of cheese on top of the bread and cover the pan with a lid. Allow the cheese to melt for about one minute. Remove the lid and take the slices off the pan with a spatula. Serve when cool.

SMILE SMOOTHIE
(GLUTEN-FREE AND VEGETARIAN)

MAKES 2 SERVINGS

YOU NEED:

- Blender
- 1 cup fresh or frozen berries
- Handful of ice cubes
- 1 cup orange juice
- 1 small yogurt (any flavor)
- 1 banana

DIRECTIONS:

1. Make sure the blender is unplugged, and dump all ingredients into the blender one by one (kids can help as long as the blender is not connected to the power source).
2. Once everything is inside and the cover is on the blender pitcher, plug in the blender and mix up the ingredients to make a cold, yummy, drinkable fruit concoction!

LUNCH

SANDWICH SHAPES

YOU NEED:

- Bread slices (white, wheat, rye, pumpernickel, etc.)
- Cookie cutters in many shapes
- Sandwich fixings (egg salad, ham and cheese, peanut butter and jelly, tuna, etc.)

DIRECTIONS:

1. Assemble the sandwiches.
2. Let the kids cut out shapes from the sandwiches using the cookie cutters. This recipe is flexible, so feel free to alter the ingredients however you want based on the child's dietary needs and restrictions.

MINI PIZZAS

YOU NEED:

- 2 or 3 English muffins or bagels
- Spaghetti sauce
- Shredded cheese
- Toppings of your choice

DIRECTIONS:

1. Preheat the oven to 400°F or turn a toaster oven on to the "bake" setting.
2. Together with the child, split open the English muffins or bagels and place them faceup on a plate.
3. Spoon some sauce over the bread until each slice is covered.
4. Take a handful of cheese and sprinkle it over the sauce.
5. Finish with a few toppings of your choice. This recipe is flexible, so feel free to alter the ingredients however you want based on the child's dietary needs and restrictions.
6. Place in toaster oven or on a cookie sheet in an oven until the cheese starts to bubble and turn golden-brown, about 5 minutes. Do not let the child approach the heat source.
7. Remove from the heat and set on a plate to cool, keeping any hot trays away from the child.

PIGS IN A BLANKET

YOU NEED:

- Hot dogs or small sausages
- Refrigerated dough
- Ketchup
- Mustard

DIRECTIONS:

1. Preheat the oven to 450°F.
2. Cut the hot dogs in half. If you are using sausage, brown it in a pan first.
3. Flatten the dough, and cut it into strips.
4. With the child's help, wrap a strip of dough around each piece of meat.
5. Put the pigs in a blanket on a cookie sheet and bake for ten minutes. Remove from the oven and allow to cool.
6. On a plate, squirt some ketchup and mustard for dipping. Serve with the pigs in a blanket.

SNAKE SALAD
(GLUTEN-FREE AND VEGETARIAN)

YOU NEED:

- Cucumber
- Zucchini
- Carrots
- Cream cheese

DIRECTIONS:

1. Carefully slice up the veggies into short pieces.
2. Spread cream cheese on one side of each slice and stick them together, arranging alternating slices of each vegetable to make a colorful snake.

DINNER

PIZZA BURGERS

MAKES 6 SERVINGS

YOU NEED:

- 1 lb. ground beef
- 1 cup melting cheese, cut into cubes
- 1 can tomato soup
- 8 rolls or hamburger buns

DIRECTIONS:

1. Cook the ground beef in a skillet over the stove until browned.
2. Add the cheese and tomato soup to the skillet. Stir slowly until the cheese is melted and the ingredients are mixed.
3. Remove from heat and allow to cool. Spoon the mixture onto the rolls, and let the kids enjoy!

CRAZY QUICHE

MAKES 8 SERVINGS

YOU NEED:

- 1 can biscuit dough
- 1 cup milk
- 3 eggs
- 1 cup shredded cheddar and mozzarella
- Sprinkle of salt and pepper
- 1 cup cubed ham (optional)
- ½ cup chopped veggies (you can use broccoli, asparagus, peppers, any vegetable you'd like!)

DIRECTIONS:

1. Preheat oven to 375°F.
2. Open the canned dough, and let the kids roll it out flat and push it into a greased pie pan. Dough is fun to play with, but make sure they don't eat it raw!
3. Bake for ten minutes until toasted a light-brown color. Remove from oven and set aside.
4. In a large bowl, let the kids beat the milk, eggs, salt, and pepper with a fork or whisk. Stir in veggies, ham (if you are using it), and shredded cheese. Pour into the prepared quiche crust.
5. Bake in preheated oven for forty-five minutes, or until eggs are set and top is golden brown.

SOUTHWEST SLOPPY JOES

MAKES 6 SERVINGS

YOU NEED:

- 1 lb. ground beef
- 1 can beans
- 1 cup salsa
- Salt and pepper
- 6 hamburger buns

DIRECTIONS:

1. Cook the ground beef in a skillet on top of the stove until it is browned.
2. Once the beef is cooked, add the beans and stir over a low heat.
3. When the meat and beans are combined, add the salsa. Cook, stirring, until the mixture is hot throughout.
4. Season with salt and pepper, and remove from heat. Allow to cool and spoon onto the rolls. Be ready with lots of napkins!

VEGETARIAN PASTA BOWL

MAKES 4 SERVINGS
YOU NEED:

- 1 lb pasta (macaroni, spirals, or ziti work best)
- 1 can tomatoes (chopped works best, but you can also use pureed)
- Dash of salt
- Pinch of basil
- An assortment of colorful bell peppers (red, green, orange, and yellow), chopped
- Shredded mozzarella (optional)
- Bread

DIRECTIONS:

1. Cook and drain the pasta according to the package's directions.
2. Put pasta back in the pot over low heat and add the can of tomatoes. Stir to combine.
3. While stirring, add salt, basil, and chopped peppers. Cook until hot throughout.
4. Add cheese and remove from heat. Serve in a bowl with some bread on the side for dipping.

SNACKS

EDIBLE SPIDERS
(VEGETARIAN)

YOU NEED:

- Creamy peanut butter
- Round crackers
- Thin stick pretzels
- Raisins

DIRECTIONS:

1. Spread peanut butter on the crackers.
2. Place four pretzel sticks on each of the crackers, arranging the pretzels so they stick out like legs.
3. Stick two of the crackers together like a sandwich. You should have an eight-legged peanut-butter cracker sandwich.
4. On the top, put two little dollops of peanut butter for eyes, and then place raisins on the peanut butter dots.

BANANA POPS
(GLUTEN-FREE AND VEGETARIAN)

YOU NEED:

- Sprinkles
- Diced nut topping
- Shredded coconut
- Mini marshmallows
- Chocolate chips
- Bananas
- Wooden sticks or skewers

DIRECTIONS:

1. Sprinkle a few teaspoons of each topping on a plate.

2. Put a handful of chocolate chips in a bowl and microwave in thirty-second increments until soft. Stir the melted chocolate around in the bowl so it's smooth.

3. Unpeel a banana, cut in half, and put a wooden stick through one end.

4. Make sure the chocolate is still warm and soft but not too hot, then have the child dip their banana into the chocolate.

5. Next, help the child roll the chocolate-covered banana into the toppings. The child can also sprinkle the toppings of their choosing over the pop instead of rolling—just make sure you place a plate underneath to catch the mess!

6. Place the finished pop on a plate and place in the freezer to cool. When cold, enjoy!

BAKE-LESS CAKE
(VEGETARIAN)

YOU NEED:

- Flat wafer cookies
- Whipped cream
- Fruit (berries, sliced apples, or bananas)
- Chocolate syrup

DIRECTIONS:

1. Start with a layer of wafer cookies on a plate. Spread cookies with whipped cream.

2. Place a few pieces of fruit on the cream and drizzle with chocolate syrup.

3. Start another layer of cookies, another layer of cream, and another layer of fruit and chocolate syrup.

4. Repeat until the cake is as tall as you want it to be.

SUNNY SALSA
(GLUTEN-FREE AND VEGAN)

MAKES 1 BOWL
YOU NEED:

- 1 large tomato
- 1 small red onion
- 1 yellow bell pepper
- 1 green bell pepper
- 1 small lime (or 1 tbsp lime juice)
- Salt and pepper
- Corn chips

DIRECTIONS:

1. Dice the tomato, peppers, and onion into tiny minced pieces. Let the kids mix them all together in a bowl until it looks like confetti.
2. Slice the lime in half and squeeze over the mixed veggies (or splash with a tablespoon of lime juice if you don't have an actual lime). Mix again and sprinkle with salt and pepper.
3. Let the salsa sit in the fridge for about an hour, then enjoy with corn chips!

BUGS ON A LOG
(GLUTEN-FREE AND VEGETARIAN)

YOU NEED:

- "Logs" made from any of these foods:
  - Celery stalks (cut to about 3 inches long)
  - Apples (cut in halves or quarters with cores removed)
  - Carrot sticks (peeled and cut to about 3 inches long)
- Spreads using any of these foods:
  - Cream cheese
  - Pimento cheese
  - Peanut butter
  - Egg salad
- "Bugs" made from any of these foods:
  - Raisins
  - Diced or dried fruit pieces
  - Chocolate chips

DIRECTIONS:

1. Top the "logs" with various spreads.
2. Give the kids some "bugs" to put on the log! If you don't need to make it gluten-free, you can also use toppings such as Cheerios, cereal fruit puffs, or broken pretzel sticks.

MAPLE APPLE TREATS
(VEGETARIAN)

MAKES 10 TREATS

YOU NEED:

- 2–3 apples
- ¼ cup cinnamon
- ¼ cup sugar
- 1 cup sour cream
- 3 tbsp maple syrup
- 10 graham crackers

DIRECTIONS:

1. Carefully cut the apples into slices and put them on a plate.
2. Mix the cinnamon and sugar together in a bowl. Let the child sprinkle some—but not all—of the cinnamon and sugar on the apples.
3. In a bowl, mix the sour cream with the syrup, and sprinkle with remaining cinnamon and sugar.
4. Spoon the mixture onto the graham crackers and top with an apple slice.

HONEY MILK BALLS
(GLUTEN-FREE AND VEGETARIAN)

MAKES 24 SMALL BALLS

YOU NEED:

- ½ cup honey or corn syrup
- 1 cup dry milk or powdered milk
- ½ cup peanut butter
- ½ cup raisins

DIRECTIONS:

1. Combine all ingredients in a bowl.
2. Mix well until too thick to stir, then knead by hand until completely blended.
3. Shape into small balls. This makes about two dozen balls.
4. Make sure you have a container ready to store the leftovers. They don't need to be refrigerated, but using an airtight container or aluminum foil wrapped over a bowl will help keep them soft.

9

BATH TIME

SCRUB-A-DUB-DUB

One of the things parents may ask you to do is to give their child a bath before bedtime. This is often part of a nighttime routine that can help children go to sleep. Routines are important for children, and babies especially can be soothed by a warm bath before bed.

It's important to have all the things you need before going into the bathroom so you do not have to get up once the child is in the water. Lay a towel on the floor of the child's room and make yourself a bath kit. Bring the bath kit into the bathroom with the child. If anything on the list is already in the bathroom, be sure it is at an arm's reach from the tub. If the parents have a cordless phone, take it into the bathroom with you as well.

Bathwater should be about 100° Fahrenheit. If you do not have a water thermometer, run the water to feel like a baby's bottle feels—warm but

not hot. Check it with your elbow or the inside of your wrist. Make sure the bathroom is comfortably warm, too, otherwise the baby might get chilly.

Remember, *never* leave a child alone in a bath. Kids can drown in just an inch of water.

INFANTS

A baby bath kit should include a clean diaper, fresh pajamas, several soft washcloths (you'll need one to soap up and wash the baby, a wet one without soap to rinse their face, a dry one to wipe their eyes if they get splashed with soap or water, and an extra one that may help entertain the baby if they try to grab at the one you're using to wash them), and a towel. The parents may provide packaged baby bath cloths that have already been soaped up. In that case, just have a dry washcloth ready in case you need to wipe soap from their eyes. You will also need baby soap or "baby bath," baby shampoo, baby oil or lotion for after the bath (if the parents desire), and a blanket (babies are usually cold after getting out of the warm water).

The parents may also ask you to add something to the baby's bathwater, such as lavender wash for relaxation or eucalyptus for a cold. Be sure you know the exact amount to add, and don't put in more than the parents tell you to. Even extra bubble bath may make a baby sick, so stick to the correct amounts for babies.

For an infant, the parents may give you a small tub or special device that goes in the big tub. Be sure to ask the parents how to use it. If you're using the big tub, make sure you wait until the water is finished running and you have checked the temperature before you put a baby in the bath.

CLEANING: Babies generally have little rolls of fat, so be sure to clean under their neck, under their arms and legs, and behind their ears. Clean between the fingers and toes (this is a good time to play "This Little Piggy" or practice counting). Use gentle motions. Wipe the baby's face with a wrung-out washcloth that was wet with only water, not soap. For the diaper area, wipe front to back on baby girls, just like you would when changing their diapers.

Remember, babies get very slippery when they're wet, so keep a hand on the baby at all times!

HAVING FUN: Once the baby is clean, let them play in the water for a little while. Be sure it is still warm and that their little feet aren't getting too pruny, which is a sign that the baby has been in the bath too long. Pruny skin can also become uncomfortable and lead to dry skin. Have fun with the baby in the water! Show the little one how to pop bubbles, make their rubber ducky float, or squirt water at them from their toy fish. You can even sing bath time songs to make it an enjoyable experience!

TODDLERS

A toddler bath kit should include a clean diaper or pull-up (whichever the child will sleep in), fresh pajamas, several soft washcloths or packaged baby bath cloths if provided, a towel, child-friendly soap, child-friendly shampoo, a cup for hair washing, and any special bath toys the child requests. Make sure you collect everything before you get into the bathroom.

A toddler can help clean themself in the bath, but you'll have to do most of the washing. Soap up two washcloths, one for you and one for the child. Guide them to each body part and gently scrub with the soapy cloth. This is also a great time to review body parts. "Where are your shoulders? Let's clean those shoulders! How about your knees?"

For a toddler's hair, you'll want to be prepared with a cup of warm water. Have the child lean back a bit and close their eyes. It helps to fold a warm, dry washcloth over their eyes during this part. Then take the cup of warm water and pour it over their hair. Soap up their head. They may want to sit up during this part. Just be sure their hair is not too drippy or the soap will run into their eyes. Once the hair is shampooed, put the cloth back over their eyes, lean them back, and rinse out the toddler's hair with more warm water in a cup. Run warm water through the child's hair as often as necessary to get rid of all the soap. If the parents provide you with a spray faucet, you may not need the cup, but be careful you don't spray in the child's eyes or use too strong a stream. Always make sure the temperature of the water remains comfortable for the child.

For a toddler, bath time is more of an adventure than a cleaning experience. They may pretend to be a pirate or a mermaid. Toddlers usually have special toys or games they look forward to using in the water. Sometimes, though, toddlers will put up a fight about taking a bath. If that happens, try talking about why it is good to take a bath, how it helps us stay clean and healthy. You can also talk about creatures that go in the water, like dolphins, sharks, and goldfish, or what you can do in the water that you can't do on "dry land" such as squirting water, playing with floating toys, making bubbles, and splashing. Let the child pick out a water creature they want to be and you can play make-believe in the bath. If you can make bath time sound fun, the child will be more likely to take a bath willingly.

Often kids refuse to take a bath because they're scared. The best way to deal with fear in little ones is to show true concern for their feelings. Use your imagination or tell them a story to help the fear go away. For example, put just a small amount of water in the tub with a few toys. Pretend it is an ocean and the child is a sailor or a mermaid. Tell them that their job is to rescue the boat or take care of a baby seal. Once they are okay with a small amount of water, add a little more (making sure the water you run into the tub is not hot).

POTTY TRAINING

Children at this age may be going through potty training. Learning to use the potty is a big step for a child. If you know the toddler is learning how to use the potty, talk to the parents about what training methods they may be using. You could have the child sit on the toilet several times throughout the day for a few minutes each time, especially right before bath time. This is good practice and often kids don't realize they have to go until they sit down. Also, remind them to try to go after eating and before going to bed.

Make sure the child flushes and washes their hands after they go. Show them how happy and proud you are! This encourages them to continue trying the new potty routine until they have it down effortlessly.

PRESCHOOL-AGE KIDS

A preschool bath kit should include fresh pajamas, fresh underwear, special age-appropriate soap and shampoo if provided, a cup for hair washing, a towel, and any requested games or toys.

By age three or four, kids generally have their bath routine down. They should be able to clean themselves, although you may have to help with the hair washing. You may not have to interact directly with them throughout the whole bath, as they may want to play with their bath toys or play make-believe alone, but do not leave the bathroom while the child is in the water.

SCHOOL-AGE KIDS

These kids are usually old enough to take a bath or shower by themselves and want their privacy, but go over the bathroom rules with the parents.

BEDTIME

NIGHT-NIGHT!

If you're working a nighttime job, you will probably have to put the children you're watching to bed. Here are some tips you might find helpful.

PUTTING A BABY TO SLEEP

A baby is too young to know it's time to go to sleep and will often oppose you. Babies have tremendously different sleep patterns than older children because they have not yet determined their sleep/wake cycles. They'll sleep if they're tired. Many parents allow babies to follow their own schedule, which means that they eat when they're hungry and sleep when they're tired. It's especially important in this situation to be able to read a baby's cues. Babies sleep often because they get tired often. When they're tired but still awake, they get cranky. Cranky babies aren't a lot of fun. It's tough on the sitter to deal with a cranky baby and it's tough on the baby themself. Look for clues that the child is tired and try to get them down for a nap before they get too cranky. This will also help prevent the baby from getting overtired. An overtired baby is even harder to get to sleep!

Some cues that a baby is tired include:

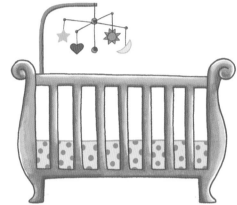

- They rub their eyes.
- They stare off into space.
- They nod off.
- They cry for no apparent reason.
- They nuzzle into your chest.
- They yawn.

A baby generally sleeps better after having a bottle. If you see the baby getting sleepy, prepare a bottle and offer it to them before putting them down for their nap or for the night. Lullabies also help to calm and relax a child into a peaceful rest. If the parents have some lullaby or classical music CDs for the baby, these are good to play at naptime or bedtime. If you know you're watching a baby, you may want to bring a classical music CD with you, or have a playlist ready on your phone. Another option you always have is singing to the baby.

When you put the baby into their crib, make sure that they are lying on their back. This is very important, as it allows the baby to breathe freely. Make sure not to put loose blankets, fluffy animals, or soft toys in bed with the baby, as these items can also restrict breathing. As long as the parents allow it, giving a baby a pacifier to sleep can help prevent them from burying their head in the blankets and keeps their airway open. It also keeps the brain active at night, as research shows that the sucking motion helps reduce the risk of SIDS, possibly by keeping the baby in a lighter stage of sleep. If the parents have pacifiers for their baby, put the baby to sleep with one and have a clean one nearby in case they spit it out and wake up.

If the child has a bumper on the crib, be sure it is tied on tightly. A crib bumper is the piece of padded fabric that you may see around the inside of the crib bars, usually tied on with five or six small strings across the bars. Bumpers are designed so the baby doesn't hit the hard wood or plastic of the crib when sleeping, but they can be dangerous. If the baby pulls the bumper off, they can get twisted in it and choke or suffocate. That is why it is important to make sure bumpers are tied on tightly.

If you've put the baby down for a nap, it's a good idea to keep the lights on and stay actively noisy. Don't be too noisy, but make general household sounds, like watching TV or talking on the phone. If the baby has gone to sleep for the evening, keep the lights off in their room and try to be very quiet. This difference in environment helps the baby distinguish between bedtime and naptime. Regardless of whether they're napping or sleeping through the night, be sure to check on the baby frequently to make sure they are still lying on their back.

Remember, if the parents give you other instructions or have specific preferences, always put their requests first. Ask if you should wake the baby up after a certain length of time for a nap. Babies generally sleep for about sixteen hours a day—usually distributed through a series of naps—and the parents may have a preferred sleep schedule for these naps. If the parents have a monitor, make sure it is turned on. A video monitor can be adjusted to point at the baby while they're in the crib. Don't worry about the light in the room. These monitors are made to pick up a clear image of the baby in dark or low light. As with any baby monitor, make sure that it is on and with you at all times so you can keep an eye on the baby while they snooze.

HOW TO PUT A TODDLER TO BED

A toddler is old enough to know about naptime or bedtime, and might also resist. Sleeping means an end to play, so resisting is natural. You can remind them that as soon as they wake up it will be a new day filled with toys, games, and fun. You can also tell them that they can play anything they want in their dreams once they've fallen asleep.

Ask the parents about the child's nighttime routine and rituals, such as picking out their pajamas, brushing their teeth, saying their prayers, or setting a cup of water on the nightstand. Find out if there is a special object, such as a blanket, a stuffed animal, or a doll that the child sleeps with. Holding onto this will help them fall asleep. It's also good to have the child hold the special nighttime object in the "getting ready for bed" time, right before they actually go to sleep. These habits help a child get ready for bed subconsciously, and make an easy transition from the parents to you, the sitter. By repeating what the parents do, you will help the child recognize a pattern. It will make them comfortable knowing that you and their parents have the same routine. If it's okay with the parents, you can sing or read bedtime stories to help the child's transition to sleep.

Sometimes it helps to pat a toddler's back until they fall asleep. Human contact is important because it helps the child understand that they are not alone and are not being abandoned while you get to stay up late and have fun. If the child is still having trouble going to sleep, you may want to try lying down next to them and pretending to fall asleep. The child may feel better about their own bedtime if they think it's your bedtime as well.

If the child still refuses to go to sleep, allow them to read or do a quiet activity in bed for a little while, as long as this is okay with the parents. This is also a good way for them to wind down and relax. Many children need to settle down and have some quiet, peaceful time before they actually fall asleep. It is best to discuss bedtime options with the parents and see what they recommend.

HOW TO DEAL WITH NIGHTMARES

If a little one wakes up crying, it is most likely from a nightmare or bad dream. Encourage the child to talk about their dream. Sometimes talking about the dream out loud will be enough to make the child feel better. If that doesn't work, try to figure out what you can do to help. For example, if the child dreamed that there was a monster under their bed, get a flashlight and look under the bed with the child to make sure there is no monster hiding there.

To help a child avoid having nightmares, it is best not to watch TV or play video games right before bedtime, especially anything with action, violence, or horror. If the child does have a nightmare, make sure you tell the parents when they get home.

SCHOOL-AGE KIDS

An older kid is more independent when going to sleep. Let them follow their own routine of changing and washing up. Remind them about an hour before bedtime that it's almost time to turn in for the night, and do quiet activities during that time. Try to avoid running around before bedtime. Once they're dressed and ready for bed, ask them if they want you to read to them. Older kids like chapter books. Try to find a calming story, not a violent, action-filled one.

If the child is having problems falling asleep, try a relaxation exercise. Tell them to close their eyes and imagine their head relaxing and going to sleep. Continue down to their toes, going from shoulders to arms to tummy to legs to feet.

Remember, your job doesn't end when the kids are asleep. Even if a child has gone to bed, they may still need you. A child may wake up because they had a bad dream or want a drink of water. Kids also get up to go to the bathroom and may need your help. Don't get wrapped up in music, video games, or anything else that may distract you from a child's call from their bedroom, and check on them every half hour to make sure they are still okay.

BABYSITTING CHILDREN WITH SPECIAL NEEDS

EXTRA CARE

You may be asked sometime in your babysitting career to watch a child with special needs such as a physical disability, hearing problem, autism, or a learning disability. You need to think about if you would be comfortable in this situation. Remember, kids are kids, no matter their age, ability, or gender, but they are also very unique. When a child has a special need, it takes a little extra knowledge, patience, understanding, and acceptance from you as the babysitter. If you do decide that you would like to take on the challenge and feel comfortable with the situation, the first step is to discuss the child's specific needs and disability with the parents.

All children are special. Children with disabilities are just as special, individual, and extraordinary as all other kids, they just have a special need that takes more focus and responsibility. Some people may call them "challenged" or "differently abled." Try not to say "disabled" or "handicapped," which may be insulting or offensive to the child and/or family. Use the words that the parents use for the child's special need.

"Special needs" does not always refer to a physical disability. The term can also refer to an emotional or mental health issue. This could include ADD, ADHD, anxiety, or bipolar disorder, just to name a few. A child with an emotional or mental disability can often look and act completely ordinary, but may be more sensitive to certain things like tags in a shirt, or have shorter attention spans than other children their age. You may need to have a longer transition time between activities and a longer winding-down time before bed. Find out the best way to avoid explosive episodes and ask about calming strategies should they be needed.

Before you accept a job, see if you can visit with the child while the parents are around to feel out the situation. This will not only give you a chance to get to know the child, but it will help them feel comfortable with you, so that they won't feel as if they've been left with a stranger when their parents go away. Be honest with the parents as to how you feel about watching the child. If you aren't comfortable with the situation, you need to tell them. Taking on a job you don't think you can handle isn't good for anyone involved.

COMMUNICATION

Communication is key to having a safe and happy time together. Learn the best way to communicate with the child. Ask how much they are able to understand, process, and remember. Some kids respond to direct eye contact whereas others may be turned off by this. Should you raise your voice, lower your voice, or talk at a steady pace? The child's parents can help fill in how best to communicate through the disability. Remember not to insult the child when communicating. Don't use baby talk just because you know they have a disability. Once you understand their level of comprehension, it will be easier to communicate at that level and not above or below it. Take their disability into consideration, but don't forget that they are still a kid who's eager to learn, play, and be an individual.

Here are some important questions to ask the parents:

- Does the child have unique or different ways of communicating, such as special words, sounds, signs, or signals? If so, what are they?

- Does the child have difficulty interacting with others? This is especially important if they will be playing with other children.
- Can the child express their needs to you, such as being hungry or having to go to the bathroom?

BEHAVIOR

Learning about the child's behavior patterns will prevent surprises and increase positive interactions between you. Children with disabilities are often disciplined in ways you may not be familiar with. For example, a child with autism may not be able to sit in a "time-out" chair after they hit their sister because they can't understand this punishment, so it's not effective. A child with a disability may process their own behavior differently and see the world differently than a child without a disability, so be sure to ask the parents the best way to deal with negative behavior.

Here are some of the things you'll want to find out about the child's behavior:

- What might they do if they get angry?
- How do they act when they're tired?
- Are there any special actions or behaviors you might see and how should you handle them?
- Does the child have any particular fears or triggers?

Ask the parents anything you can think of. As with all children, the more information you can gather the more enjoyable your time together will be.

PLAYTIME

Kids with disabilities are still able to play, just in different ways. They may be into a different kind of toy or game, or have special tools they need to use.

Find out what the child's likes and dislikes are so you can design games around what they like. For example, if they really love knights and castles, you can play a make-believe game where they're a prince or princess in a castle—ask about their kingdom and pet dragon. Or you may find out they love coloring—you can rip up a paper bag, break out the crayons, and have an awesome coloring fest!

Some of the things you'll want to find out about the child's play habits:

- Does the child have any special play routines?
- Do they have any specific play-assistance equipment? If so, find out how it works.
- What toys and games does the child prefer?
- Is there anything specific that calms them down if they're upset?
- How closely do they need to be supervised, and how much help will they need? It may seem like the six-year-old you're watching can climb up the slide's ladder just fine, but their disability may interfere with their balance or confidence.

Ask parents tons of questions, and ask them to be specific with their answers. And above all else, be positive, be patient, and be respectful!

12

PROBLEMS YOU MAY ENCOUNTER

SHOULD I BABYSIT A SICK CHILD?

Often parents need a babysitter when a child is sick because a daycare or preschool won't take them. If you're out of school during a holiday or in the summer, you may be asked to watch a child who is ill.

First decide if that is a responsibility you want to take on. It is best to babysit after the first day or two of illness, after they see the doctor. Remember, a sick child is cranky and needy when they're not feeling well, and they require extra patience, sensitivity, and understanding. Also, they can be contagious. Before you babysit, ask the parents what illness the child has, if they are contagious, if they have been to the doctor yet, and what care is needed.

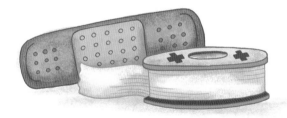

Remember to be extra tolerant with a sick child—they will probably be grouchy, and could use some tender loving care.

WHAT HAPPENS IF THE NONCUSTODIAL PARENT COMES OVER DEMANDING TO TAKE THE CHILDREN?

What is the noncustodial parent? This is a parent that does not have legal custody of the child or children that you are babysitting. Custody means the right and responsibility to care for a child. Generally, divorced parents have joint custody, but if one parent does not have the legal authority to see their children, the parent who hired you should tell you. Ask them what procedure they want you to follow if the other parent shows up (such as calling a neighbor, their attorney, or the police). Taking a child away from the parent who has custody is a criminal offense.

If the parent comes to the house and you were told that they do not have custody, access, or visitation, do not let the parent inside. Most noncustodial parents do not have the keys to their ex's house. Call the custodial parent right away and ask how they want you to proceed. If the noncustodial parent begins to harass or threaten you, call the police.

If the parent does have access to the house, do not physically try to stop the parent from taking the children. You and/or the children could be hurt in the process. Follow the instructions that the custodial parent gave you and call them right away.

IF YOU SUSPECT CHILD ABUSE

If you think a child is being abused, report it right away. Contact your local authorities or call a national child abuse hotline (such as, in the United States, Childhelp, (1-800) 4-A-CHILD). It's okay if you don't have any proof of abuse—it's not your job to prove it. You should be looking out for the best interests of the child. As long as you are honestly concerned, report suspected abuse or neglect immediately. You may save a child's life.

Write down as much information as you can about the child and family and the suspected abuse before you make the call. Include the names of the children and parents, their address, phone number, and how you know the family. Do you think the abuse is physical, emotional, sexual, or neglect? Write down examples of the suspected abuse, such as bruises, drawings of abuse, unnatural fears, or something the child told you. Make the phone call from your home and be prepared with a pen and paper to write down any information you are given. You may want to explain the situation to your parents and have them sit with you when you make the call. It is always helpful to involve an adult that you trust.

Many cities or towns have their own abuse hotline or reporting number. Contact your local Child and Family Services, Child Protective Services, or Social Services for assistance and further details. If you cannot find these numbers, call your local police and ask them for the number to report possible child abuse. Remember to stay calm and honest, and speak slowly and clearly on the phone. If you wish to remain anonymous, be sure you tell them.

NATURAL DISASTERS

What are natural disasters? These emergency situations are a form of extremely harsh weather, such as a tornado or hurricane. Extreme weather can be very destructive and scary, especially when you're babysitting. Learning how to prepare for and deal with these disasters can help reduce the risk of both injuries and fear. Children may be especially frightened during such an overpowering event since their parents are not there. Remind the child that you'll be there for them and will look out for them until their parents are able to come home. If the child is scared of the storm, ease their fear with a story about the weather. Read some mythological tales about storms, explain why it rains from a scientific point of view, or tell a story about magical winds and miraculous thunderclaps. Whether the story is fiction or nonfiction, story time can help ease a child's fears and redirect their attention.

Be sure you call the child's parents during any threatening disaster. They may have an emergency plan for you to follow, such as going to a neighbor's house or having a friend pick you up. If you discussed a plan previously, be prepared to follow through with the instructions you were given.

STAYING INFORMED

If you hear of a watch or warning, whether it's on the radio, TV, or from a cell phone alert:

- Shut all doors and windows.
- If it's safe to remain in the living room, keep the radio or TV on to listen for updates.
- Keep your cell phone on you and check frequently for updates, texts, and news briefings.

Some natural disasters you may encounter are:

TORNADOES: A watch tells you a tornado is possible and may be coming, while a warning tells you it is coming and you need to take action. When you hear there is a tornado warning, immediately go to the storm shelter, basement, or lowest part of the house with the children. If you can't find a room without windows, go to the center of a small room, such as the bathroom or a closet, as far away from the windows as possible, and sit on the floor with the kids. If there is a table nearby, pull it into the center of the room and sit under the table.

HURRICANES: If you're not told to evacuate, stay indoors! Get a flashlight and turn off any electrical devices you had been using, such as the computer. Collect some play items that you can easily carry, like coloring books and crayons, storybooks, or a stuffed animal, and go to the storm shelter, basement, or lowest part of the house with the children. If you are in a room that has windows, go to the center of the room, as far away from the windows as possible, and sit on the floor with the kids. If you are told there is an evacuation of your area, dress yourself and the children in rain gear—long cotton shirts and pants, hats, raincoats, and rain boots. Don't take an umbrella because the high winds will tear it away. If you cannot reach the parents by phone, leave them a note in the house as well as a voicemail or text saying where you are going and with whom. Then head to the closest neighbor and follow them in the direction of evacuation.

FLOODS: If you are told there is an evacuation of your area, leave immediately. If you cannot reach the parents by phone, leave them a note in the house and a voicemail or text saying where you are going and with whom. Flooding happens very fast. Head to the closest neighbor and follow them in the direction of evacuation to higher ground. If you walk into water any deeper than your ankles turn around and go another way. Do not let the children try to play in the water. Standing water and deep water can be very dangerous. Never drive in standing water.

VOLCANOES: Close all windows, air vents, or anything leading to the outdoors (such as a chimney flue) so the ash will not enter the house. If you are told there is an evacuation for your area, be sure to listen to the details of the evacuation plan. It is important to know which direction to go. Dress yourself and the children in the most protective outfits you can find, such as cotton pants, long-sleeve shirts, and hats. Falling ash is made up of tiny little pieces of rock and glass and can be very harmful to a person's lungs. Grab damp cloths to put over your noses and mouths to protect yourself and the kids from breathing in the ash. Help children younger than two years old hold the cloth. If you cannot reach the parents by phone, leave them a note in the house and a voicemail or text saying where you are going and with whom. Then head to the closest neighbor and follow them in the direction of evacuation.

WILDFIRES: If you are told there is an evacuation of your area, dress yourself and the children in the most protective outfits you can find, such as cotton pants, long-sleeve shirts, hiking boots or sturdy shoes with thick soles, and hats. If you cannot reach the parents by phone, leave them a note in the house and a voicemail or text saying where you are going and with whom. Then head to the closest neighbor and follow them in the direction of evacuation.

While waiting out the weather, you can play make-believe games, sing songs, or tell stories. If the child is old enough to understand what is going on, reassure them that you will do everything you can to protect them.

Remember that not all natural disasters occur in every part of the country. Become familiar with the type of extreme weather your area has and discuss emergency plans with the parents of the children you are watching.

CONCLUSION

- - - - - - - -

Congratulations on finishing *The Babysitter's Survival Guide*!

You have taken a fantastic step toward gaining more knowledge about safety, creativity, and child development. Not only will this help you become a better babysitter, it will also help you grow as a person and become more mature, resourceful, and independent.

Remember that the information you've learned in this guide may not apply to every babysitting situation. It's important to talk to the parents about their children, their home, and what they expect from you. You have acquired some great skills, and every babysitting job you take on will make you a better babysitter!

Bring this book with you when you go to your sitting jobs. You can refer to it for crafts, recipes, and safety questions, and take notes about the kids you watch.

Now score those jobs, get those art projects ready, and have fun with the kids!

Best of luck,

Jill

BIBLIOGRAPHY

Bowlby, John. *Attachment: Attachment and Loss*, Vol. 1. New York, NY: Basic Books, 1969.

Broderick, Patricia C., and Pamela Blewitt. *The Life Span: Human Development for Helping Professionals.* Upper Saddle River, NJ: Merrill/Prentice Hall, 2003.

Garner, Pamela W., and Thomas G. Power. "Preschoolers' Emotional Control in the Disappointment Paradigm and Its Relation to Temperament, Emotional Knowledge, and Family Expressiveness." *Child Development* 67, no. 4 (August 1996): 1406–1419.

Hammer, Melina. *Kid Chef: The Foodie Kids Cookbook: Healthy Recipes and Culinary Skills for the New Cook in the Kitchen.* Berkeley, CA: Sonoma Press, 2016.

Hetherington, E. M., and Ross D. Parke. *Child Psychology: A Contemporary Viewpoint*, 5th ed. New York, NY: McGraw-Hill, 2003.

Jana, Laura A., and Jennifer Shu. *Heading Home with Your Newborn: From Birth to Reality.* Elk Grove Village, IL: American Academy of Pediatrics, 2010.

Siegel, Daniel J., and Tina P. Bryson. *The Whole-Brain Child: 12 Revolutionary Strategies to Nurture Your Child's Developing Mind.* New York, NY: Bantam Books, 2012.

Small, Lindsey. *Card Games for Kids: 36 of the Best Card Games for Children and Families.* Surrey, England: Small Publishing, Ltd., 2014.

Wels, Kelly. *Changing Diapers: The Hip Mom's Guide to Modern Cloth Diapering.* Waterford, ME: Green Team Enterprises, 2012.

ABOUT THE AUTHOR

JILL D. CHASSÉ has been working with children for over twenty years. In high school she was the president of the Babysitters Club of Cedar Grove, coordinating part-time childcare and summer play activities. After high school, she began teaching at child development centers and became director of her first center in 1998. Dr. Chassé ran the Club Mom program at a child play center and taught the Department of Education's Balls and Ramps program in Maryland.

After college, she became a consultant to numerous child-development centers, assisting with curriculum development, teacher training, and licensure requirements. She received education in midwifery and pregnancy counseling and has worked closely with parents regarding perinatal mental health and child development issues for over fifteen years. After having her children, Dr. Chassé went on to earn a master's degree in public administration and a master's degree in psychology, concentrating in developmental and family psychology. Additionally, she holds a PhD in psychology and health administration and a Doctor of Public Health degree focusing on maternal/perinatal epidemiology. Currently, Dr. Chassé works as a public health practitioner, mommy, and writer, and lives in the New York metropolitan area with her family.

INDEX

A

Activities and crafts
    about: drawing with children, 59;
        make-believe guns, 55; over-
        view and planning, 54–55
    arts and crafts, 56–60
    for elementary schoolers, 31–33,
        35–36
    for infants (newborn to one year),
        24–27
    for kids of all ages, 55–66
    kitchen projects, 62–66
    for preschoolers, 30–31
    seasonal creations, 60–61
    special-needs kids and, 92–93
    for toddlers, 27–29
Advertising, 6–8
Age groups. *See* Elementary
    schoolers; Infants; Preschoolers;
    Toddlers

B

Babysitting jobs. *See also* Infor-
    mation to know (before parents
    leave); Safety
    arriving on time, 14
    comforting kids, 37–47
    getting home after, 21
    interviewing for. *See* Interviews
    leaving the house, 21
    making good impression, 14
    parents late coming home, 19–20,
        21
    payment for, 19. *See also* Hourly
        rates
    what to wear, 13
Bathing kids, 20, 81–84

Bedtime, 21, 43, 85–89
Business cards, 6–7, 111–113
Business of babysitting. *See also*
    Hourly rates
    advertising, 6–8
    requirements for, 1
    resume for, 2–4

C

Child abuse, suspecting, 95–96
Child information sheets, 15–16,
    115–119
Clothing, what to wear, 9, 13
Comforting kids, 37–47
    first aid/CPR and, 5, 38–41
    infants, 41–45
    pre-school/school-age kids,
        46–47
    toddlers, 46
    when dad and mom leave, 37–38
Co-op babysitting, 21
CPR/First aid, 5
Crying, 27, 37–38, 41–45, 46, 88. *See*
    also Comforting kids

D

Diapers, changing, 21, 42
Disabilities. *See* Special-needs
    children
Door, answering, 19, 20

E

Elementary schoolers (age 5-10)
    activities for, 31–33, 35–36
    bathing, 84
    comforting, 47
    fighting, 50–51

    putting to bed, 88–89
    what to expect, 31, 33–35
Emergency information, 14–15,
    121–123

F

Fighting, 48–53
Fire safety, 18, 98
First aid/CPR, 5, 38–41
Floods, 97
Flyers, 6, 7
Food and feeding
    about: general guidelines, 67
    breakfast recipes, 71–72
    crying babies and, 43
    dinner recipes, 75–77
    food restrictions and allergies,
        67–68
    infants, 68–69
    lunch recipes, 73–75
    older kids, 69–70
    safety precautions, 68, 70
    snack recipes, 77–80

H

Homework rules, 17
Hourly rates
    determining, 5
    discussing in interview, 12, 21
    doing extra work and, 12
    getting paid, 19
    special charges, 12, 21–22
    for vacation babysitting, 21–22
House rules, 16–19. *See also* Infor-
    mation to know (before parents
    leave)
Hurricanes, 97

I

Infants (newborn to one year)
  activities for, 24–27
  bathing, 81–83
  crying, comforting, 27, 37–38,
    41–45
  feeding, 68–69
  holding babies, 24
  putting to sleep, 85–87
  rhythmic movement and sounds, 43
  sucking reflex, 44
  swaddling, 44–45
  touching tenderly, 44
  what to expect, 22–27
Information to know (before parents leave). See also Safety
  homework rules, 17
  house layout (walk-through), 16
  house rules, 16–19
  picture taking, 18
  screen time, 17–18
  telephone rules, 19
Interviews, 9–12
  co-op babysitting, nanny-shares
    and, 21
  finding out about children, 10
  getting to know parents, 10
  location of, 12
  other important points to discuss,
    10–12
  precautions, 12
  questions to ask, 10
  summary points to remember, 9
  vacation babysitting and, 21–22

N

Nanny-shares, 21
Natural disasters, 96–98
Nightmares, 88
Noncustodial parents, 95

P

Pictures, taking, 18
Potty training, 84
Preschoolers (ages 3–4)
  activities for, 30–31
  bathing, 81–82, 84
  comforting, 46–47
  fighting, 49–50
  positive role model for, 30
  putting to bed, 88–89
  what to expect, 29–30
Punishment, 52–53

R

Rates. See Hourly rates
Recipes, 71–80
References, 2–3
Resume, 2–4
Role model, being, 30
Rules, 16–19. See also Information
  to know (before parents leave)

S

Safety
  answering the door, 19, 20
  bathing, 81–82
  child information sheets and,
    15–16, 115–119
  emergency information, 15–16,
    121–123
  fire safety, 18, 98
  first aid/CPR, 5, 38–41
  food and cooking, 68, 70
  importance of, 14
  knowing address of where you
    are, 14
  natural disasters, 96–98
  parents late coming home and,
    19–20, 21
  sucking reflex and SIDS, 44

  suspecting child abuse, 95–96
  tips, for after parents have left,
    20–21
Schedule form, 107–110
School-aged kids. See Elementary
  schoolers
Screen time, 17–18
Sibling rivalry, 51
Sick children, 94
Social media, 8, 18
Special-needs children, 90–93
Swaddling, 44–45

T

Telephone rules, 19
Temper tantrums and fighting,
  48–53
Toddlers (ages 1–2)
  activities for, 27–29
  bathing, 81–82, 83–84
  behaving badly (terrible twos),
    28–29
  comforting, 46
  fighting, 48–49
  potty training, 84
  putting to bed, 87–88
  what to expect, 27, 28–29
Tornados, 97
TV and screen time, 17–18

V

Vacation babysitting, 21–22
Volcanoes, 97–98

W

Walker precaution, 20
Walk-through of house, 16
Websites, 7
Word-of-mouth advertising, 8

BABYSITTING SCHEDULES

Use these pages to help keep your babysitting jobs in order.

Date of Job:

Start Time: .... End Time: ....

Parents' Names:

Kids' Names:

Hourly Rate:

How will I get there/home?:

Date of Job:

Start Time: .... End Time: ....

Parents' Names:

Kids' Names:

Hourly Rate:

How will I get there/home?:

Date of Job:

Start Time: .... End Time: ....

Parents' Names:

Kids' Names:

Hourly Rate:

How will I get there/home?:

Date of Job: ....

Start Time: .... End Time: ....

Parents' Names: ....

Kids' Names: ....

Hourly Rate: ....

How will I get there/home?: ....

Date of Job: ....

Start Time: .... End Time: ....

Parents' Names: ....

Kids' Names: ....

Hourly Rate: ....

How will I get there/home?: ....

Date of Job: ....

Start Time: .... End Time: ....

Parents' Names: ....

Kids' Names: ....

Hourly Rate: ....

How will I get there/home?: ....

Date of Job: ....

Start Time: .... End Time: ....

Parents' Names: ....

Kids' Names: ....

Hourly Rate: ....

How will I get there/home?: ....

Date of Job: ....

Start Time: .... End Time: ....

Parents' Names: ....

Kids' Names: ....

Hourly Rate: ....

How will I get there/home?: ....

Date of Job: ....

Start Time: .... End Time: ....

Parents' Names: ....

Kids' Names: ....

Hourly Rate: ....

How will I get there/home?: ....

Date of Job: ....

Start Time: .... End Time: ....

Parents' Names: ....

Kids' Names: ....

Hourly Rate: ....

How will I get there/home?: ....

Date of Job: ....

Start Time: .... End Time: ....

Parents' Names: ....

Kids' Names: ....

Hourly Rate: ....

How will I get there/home?: ....

Date of Job:

Start Time: End Time:

Parents' Names:

Kids' Names:

Hourly Rate:

How will I get there/home?:

Date of Job:

Start Time: End Time:

Parents' Names:

Kids' Names:

Hourly Rate:

How will I get there/home?:

Date of Job:

Start Time: End Time:

Parents' Names:

Kids' Names:

Hourly Rate:

How will I get there/home?:

Date of Job:

Start Time: End Time:

Parents' Names:

Kids' Names:

Hourly Rate:

How will I get there/home?:

MAKE YOUR OWN BUSINESS CARDS!

Fill in the blanks on the perforated cards below to make your own babysitting business cards!

BABYSITTING SERVICE

Name:

Experience:

Age:

Cell number:

E-mail:

BABYSITTING SERVICE

Name:

Experience:

Age:

Cell number:

E-mail:

BABYSITTING SERVICE

Name:

Experience:

Age:

Cell number:

E-mail:

BABYSITTING SERVICE

Name:

Experience:

Age:

Cell number:

E-mail:

BABYSITTING SERVICE

Name:

Experience:

Age:

Cell number:

E-mail:

BABYSITTING SERVICE

Name:

Experience:

Age:

Cell phone number:

E-mail:

BABYSITTING SERVICE

Name:

Experience:

Age:

Cell number:

E-mail:

BABYSITTING SERVICE

Name:

Experience:

Age:

Cell number:

E-mail:

MAKE YOUR OWN BUSINESS CARDS!

Fill in the blanks on the perforated cards below to make your own babysitting business cards!

BABYSITTING SERVICE

Name:

Experience:

Age:

Cell number:

E-mail:

BABYSITTING SERVICE

Name:

Experience:

Age:

Cell number:

E-mail:

BABYSITTING SERVICE

Name:

Experience:

Age:

Cell number:

E-mail:

BABYSITTING SERVICE

Name:

Experience:

Age:

Cell number:

E-mail:

BABYSITTING SERVICE

Name:

Experience:

Age:

Cell number:

E-mail:

BABYSITTING SERVICE

Name:

Experience:

Age:

Cell phone number:

E-mail:

BABYSITTING SERVICE

Name:

Experience:

Age:

Cell number:

E-mail:

BABYSITTING SERVICE

Name:

Experience:

Age:

Cell number:

E-mail:

CHILD INFORMATION SHEETS

Child's name:

Nickname(s):

Date of birth: Age:

Allergies:

Medications:

Special instructions:

Naptime: Bedtime:

Mealtimes: (B)   (L)   (D)

Are snacks okay?: [Y] [N]

Favorite activities:

Favorite songs:

Favorite toys:

Friends:

Other notes:

Child's name:

Nickname(s):

Date of birth: Age:

Allergies:

Medications:

Special instructions:

Naptime: Bedtime:

Mealtimes: (B)   (L)   (D)

Are snacks okay?: [Y] [N]

Favorite activities:

Favorite songs:

Favorite toys:

Friends:

Other notes:

Child's name:

Nickname(s):

Date of birth: Age:

Allergies:

Medications:

Special instructions:

Naptime: Bedtime:

Mealtimes: (B)   (L)   (D)

Are snacks okay?: [Y] [N]

Favorite activities:

Favorite songs:

Favorite toys:

Friends:

Other notes:

Child's name:

Nickname(s):

Date of birth: Age:

Allergies:

Medications:

Special instructions:

Naptime: Bedtime:

Mealtimes: (B)   (L)   (D)

Are snacks okay?: [Y] [N]

Favorite activities:

Favorite songs:

Favorite toys:

Friends:

Other notes:

CHILD INFORMATION SHEETS

Child's name: ....

Nickname(s): ....

Date of birth: .... Age: ....

Allergies: ....

Medications: ....

Special instructions: ....

Naptime: .... Bedtime: ....

Mealtimes: (B) .... (L) .... (D) ....

Are snacks okay?: [Y] [N]

Favorite activities: ....

Favorite songs: ....

Favorite toys: ....

Friends: ....

Other notes: ....

Child's name: ....

Nickname(s): ....

Date of birth: .... Age: ....

Allergies: ....

Medications: ....

Special instructions: ....

Naptime: .... Bedtime: ....

Mealtimes: (B) .... (L) .... (D) ....

Are snacks okay?: [Y] [N]

Favorite activities: ....

Favorite songs: ....

Favorite toys: ....

Friends: ....

Other notes: ....

Child's name: ....

Nickname(s): ....

Date of birth: .... Age: ....

Allergies: ....

Medications: ....

Special instructions: ....

Naptime: .... Bedtime: ....

Mealtimes: (B) .... (L) .... (D) ....

Are snacks okay?: [Y] [N]

Favorite activities: ....

Favorite songs: ....

Favorite toys: ....

Friends: ....

Other notes: ....

Child's name: ....

Nickname(s): ....

Date of birth: .... Age: ....

Allergies: ....

Medications: ....

Special instructions: ....

Naptime: .... Bedtime: ....

Mealtimes: (B) .... (L) .... (D) ....

Are snacks okay?: [Y] [N]

Favorite activities: ....

Favorite songs: ....

Favorite toys: ....

Friends: ....

Other notes: ....

CHILD INFORMATION SHEETS

Child's name: ....

Nickname(s): ....

Date of birth: .... Age: ....

Allergies: ....

Medications: ....

Special instructions: ....

Naptime: .... Bedtime: ....

Mealtimes: (B) .... (L) .... (D) ....

Are snacks okay?: [Y] [N]

Favorite activities: ....

Favorite songs: ....

Favorite toys: ....

Friends: ....

Other notes: ....

Child's name: ....

Nickname(s): ....

Date of birth: .... Age: ....

Allergies: ....

Medications: ....

Special instructions: ....

Naptime: .... Bedtime: ....

Mealtimes: (B) .... (L) .... (D) ....

Are snacks okay?: [Y] [N]

Favorite activities: ....

Favorite songs: ....

Favorite toys: ....

Friends: ....

Other notes: ....

Child's name: ....

Nickname(s): ....

Date of birth: .... Age: ....

Allergies: ....

Medications: ....

Special instructions: ....

Naptime: .... Bedtime: ....

Mealtimes: (B) .... (L) .... (D) ....

Are snacks okay?: [Y] [N]

Favorite activities: ....

Favorite songs: ....

Favorite toys: ....

Friends: ....

Other notes: ....

Child's name: ....

Nickname(s): ....

Date of birth: .... Age: ....

Allergies: ....

Medications: ....

Special instructions: ....

Naptime: .... Bedtime: ....

Mealtimes: (B) .... (L) .... (D) ....

Are snacks okay?: [Y] [N]

Favorite activities: ....

Favorite songs: ....

Favorite toys: ....

Friends: ....

Other notes: ....

EMERGENCY INFORMATION SHEETS

Family's name: ....

Children's name(s): ....

Address: ....

....

Nearest cross streets: ....

Parents' phone numbers: ....

Emergency contact name and phone number: ....

....

Police / fire department: ....

Hospital: ....

Doctor's name and phone number: ....

....

Poison Control Center: ....

Family's name: ....

Children's name(s): ....

Address: ....

....

Nearest cross streets: ....

Parents' phone numbers: ....

Emergency contact name and phone number: ....

....

Police / fire department: ....

Hospital: ....

Doctor's name and phone number: ....

....

Poison Control Center: ....

Family's name: ....

Children's name(s): ....

Address: ....

....

Nearest cross streets: ....

Parents' phone numbers: ....

Emergency contact name and phone number: ....

....

Police / fire department: ....

Hospital: ....

Doctor's name and phone number: ....

....

Poison Control Center: ....

Family's name: ....

Children's name(s): ....

Address: ....

....

Nearest cross streets: ....

Parents' phone numbers: ....

Emergency contact name and phone number: ....

....

Police / fire department: ....

Hospital: ....

Doctor's name and phone number: ....

....

Poison Control Center: ....

EMERGENCY INFORMATION SHEETS

Family's name: ....

Children's name(s): ....

Address: ....

....

Nearest cross streets: ....

Parents' phone numbers: ....

Emergency contact name and phone number: ....

....

Police / fire department: ....

Hospital: ....

Doctor's name and phone number: ....

....

Poison Control Center: ....

Family's name: ....

Children's name(s): ....

Address: ....

....

Nearest cross streets: ....

Parents' phone numbers: ....

Emergency contact name and phone number: ....

....

Police / fire department: ....

Hospital: ....

Doctor's name and phone number: ....

....

Poison Control Center: ....

Family's name: ....

Children's name(s): ....

Address: ....

....

Nearest cross streets: ....

Parents' phone numbers: ....

Emergency contact name and phone number: ....

....

Police / fire department: ....

Hospital: ....

Doctor's name and phone number: ....

....

Poison Control Center: ....

Family's name: ....

Children's name(s): ....

Address: ....

....

Nearest cross streets: ....

Parents' phone numbers: ....

Emergency contact name and phone number: ....

....

Police / fire department: ....

Hospital: ....

Doctor's name and phone number: ....

....

Poison Control Center: ....